The Canoe Yawl

The Canoe Yawl

From the birth of leisure sailing to the 21st century

RICHARD POWELL

Lodestar Books

Published 2016 by
Lodestar Books
71 Boveney Road, London, SE23 3NL, United Kingdom
lodestarbooks.com

A CIP catalogue record for this book is available from the British Library

ISBN 978-1-907206-31-3

Typeset by Lodestar Books
in Equity and Concourse typefaces designed by Matthew Butterick

Printed in Spain by Graphy Cems, Navarra
All papers used by Lodestar Books are sourced responsibly

FSC
www.fsc.org
MIX
Paper from responsible sources
FSC® C007507

Contents

To Sara,
for her patience

Foreword

THE CANOE-YAWL HAS A LONG AND FASCINATING HISTORY. Unlike most modern boats, the evolution can be traced, as it is here, from working boats, which of course had to be able and seaworthy, to leisure craft, which at the time were just beginning to become popular.

The development sheered off in various directions: the small paddling 'Rob Roy' type sprouted sails, and began to be raced, which inevitably, over a long period, led to serious racing craft, the ultimate example being the spectacular International 10 Square Metre class, which is still popular. While the small paddling, and sailing/paddling canoes are still very familiar, as they have been for well over 100 years, especially in Britain and America.

Meanwhile many more substantial vessels emerged, like the one we see on the cover. These were capable of more serious cruising, and early on made some remarkable voyages, being shipped across to the continent and exploring canals, coastal inlets, estuaries, rivers; many interesting hidden places which larger deeper boats can never find their way into.

The larger boats were built with minimal cuddies and cabins, which made them more habitable. These also remain popular, perhaps becoming more so, having several notable advantages for trailerability, ease of handling, shallow draught, and overall seaworthiness.

The author progresses on to deep-keel yawls; although reluctant to be too specific in definitions, some may feel that a centreboarder is a canoe-yawl, and a deep ballast keel makes a canoe-yacht. I however will not complain about several of the latter type appearing here: especially some of Albert Strange's timeless classics, like the *Sheila* and the *Norma*. Richard uses the term 'Canoe Yawl' in a loose and all-embracing sense. There are, however, double-ended yawl-rigged craft of different styles; it may be difficult to pin them down with definitions, but they simply do not look like Canoe Yawls!

Now what is so good about Canoe Yawls? As with other wooden boats, they offer a welcome and necessary relief from modern production boats, with their cold hard shiny slippery glary white plastic.

And the freedom to build, or have built, a boat which is designed, set up and refined for the sailor's particular needs and fancies in construction, finish, layout, and sailing rig.

This yawl rig is a particularly user-friendly rig; the spars are short, the centre of effort is low, and the rig is quickly and easily shortened down or adjusted according to the conditions. In a sudden hard gust, the boat, although heeling considerably, will remain balanced on the helm, and will not screw up into the wind in the way a tall bermuda rig is inclined to do. If the lively breeze persists, the mainsail may be lowered, and the boat remains well-balanced and handy. Or by trimming the jib and mizzen sheets the boat may keep way on, well under control, while a reef or two are tucked in.

The double-ended hull has a lot to do with this good behaviour, especially with a short-ended hull, maintaining a healthy balance of buoyancy fore-and-aft.

These boats have a comfortable and reassuring quality, which we—those of us who find the style appealing—find pleasant to live with, eminently able, safe, and practical in use, and good to look at.

Iain Oughtred
Isle of Skye
May 2016

1 Four Pioneers

THE INDEPENDENCE OF THOUGHT and questing mind which gave rise to the canoe yawl were prefigured and personified by four Victorian pioneers of leisure boating: R. T. McMullen, John MacGregor, James Gordon and Lt. E. E. Middleton, all of whom made ambitious voyages and lived to record them in popular accounts of the time.

* * *

Richard Turrell McMullen was born around 1830 at Stockwell, now in Greater London but then part of Surrey; his parents are unknown, but he did have a brother, identified as J. McMullen. The family must have been fairly wealthy as his brother studied Law at the Inns of Court and Richard became a member of the Stock Exchange in 1853. He married, Emily, 8 years his junior, at the end of 1858. It is believed he lived mainly in Greenhithe on the Kent shore of the lower Thames, but later moved and in 1881 was living in Swanscombe, Kent.

McMullen was strongly protestant and conservative, believing profoundly in individual responsibility, and was very much against the trade union movement. He wrote extensively on religious matters as well as sailing. He had a passionate interest in astronomy and the delights of a starry night feature many times in his writing, in fact all his boats were named after stars or constellations. He also expressed strong dislikes in respect of screw steamers, early mechanically propelled vehicles and attempts at flying; it may therefore come as no surprise that he also defended the literal interpretation of the Book of Genesis in a very robust and inventive manner.

He began the then unusual activity of cruising under sail in 1850, and fortunately for us recorded his activities in some detail. In the early days he averaged 1000 miles

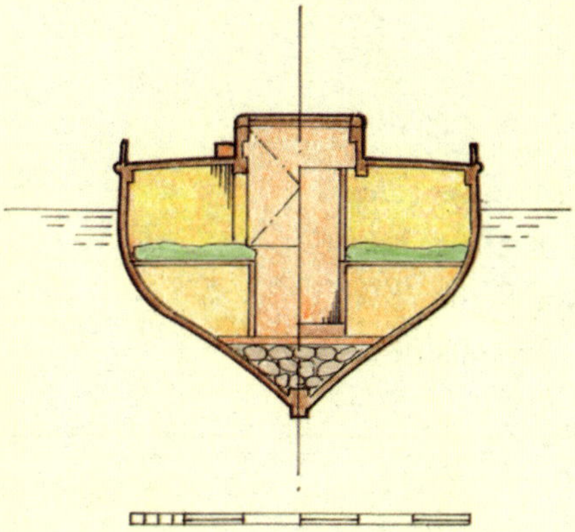

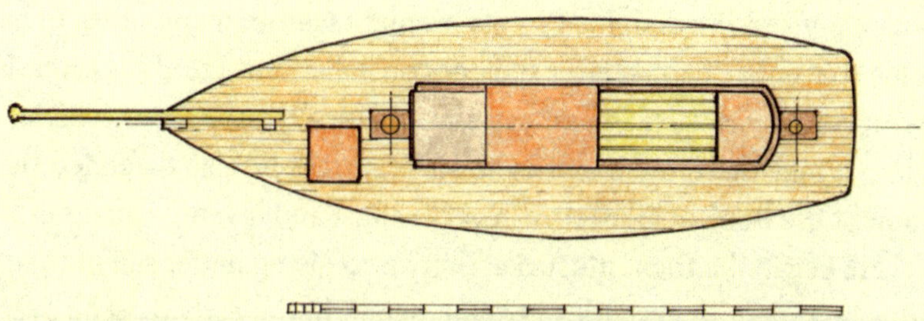

LEO, 1850

Built by J. Thompson of Rotherhithe; 2.5 tons BM; LOA 20ft; LWL 18ft; beam 6ft. 3in; draught 4ft. Ballast was 23 cwt. and the sail area about 280 sq. ft. inc.topsail.

a year, and by 1858 this had risen to 1800 miles; he also completed a circumnavigation of England, Scotland & Wales, some 2640 miles, in 1863. He was very thorough and meticulous in the preparation of his boats prior to a cruise, and with his seamanship during the passage. He was the first man to advocate staying at sea in small boats in a gale, recognising the difference between small and light draft, and the absolute necessity of good seamanship for the boat's survival. He paid very detailed attention to the forces of the sea acting on the vessel in shoals and tide races, a consideration new to recreational sailing, and previously the closely guarded domain of fishermen and other working sailors.

He owned a number of boats during his lifetime, modified several of his earlier ones, and developed later designs based on his own experiences, constantly adapting them to suit his purpose. He usually sailed with a crew but also did a fair amount of single-handed cruising, a couple of his boats being designed with this in mind. The first that he owned was the little cutter *Leo*, a very small yacht indeed for her time. She was built at Rotherhithe, of pine, in 1850. The use of pine indicates fairly cheap construction, which is partly confirmed by her being re-fastened and having her deck replaced in 1856. That said, she had a hard life, cruising extensively every year.

Measurements, including a mid-ship section, were taken from a Revenue cutter on the hard at Rotherhithe in 1849 and divided by three. *Leo* was one of the earliest purpose designed cruisers, but this scaling down, although expedient at the time, is fraught with difficulty. A midship section suitable for a 54ft. LWL vessel is woefully lacking in stiffness and freeboard for one of 18ft LWL. She had only 9in. freeboard at the quarters plus a 4in. rail. This is a recipe for a very wet boat and a regular dip in the water if one is not very careful. This happened to McMullen at least once and apparently turned his brother off sailing for life, on only his second trip.

She was half decked initially and consequently sank on the night following her launch, and a second mishap prompted him to have her fully decked, which was carried out immediately afterwards. McMullen then considered her to be 'safe and seaworthy'. She was still very tender and the fact that he sailed the 8000-odd miles during the seven years he owned her, taking her as far as Lands End on one occasion without managing to drown himself, reflects much credit. It has to be said that it was more a tribute to his thoroughness in preparation and good seamanship than to his elementary knowledge of yacht design.

His next boat was *Sirius*, by the same builder and to the same lines as *Leo* but with a 50% increase in the dimensions. The next, *Orion*, was similar but with the dimensions further increased. The last two were single-handers; interestingly both had a yawl rig, which McMullen had adopted following the lengthening of *Orion*. The first of these, *Procyon*, was built in 1867 at Whitstable, lengthened in 1870 to 28ft. 6in. LOA with a 7ft. 9in. beam. She was a carefully thought out design and incorporated a ¾in. thick steel centreplate, 10ft. long with an 18in. drop. His final boat was *Perseus*, built in 1890, again at Whitstable; she was a little lighter than *Procyon* with increased ballast and carried a bowsprit with a small jib. She was also fitted out with all the latest equipment for his creature comforts and ease of use.

McMullen cruised extensively all his life, and when he died, aged 61, on 14 June 1891 it was (fittingly, he might have thought) at the tiller of *Perseus*: he was found dead at the helm, mid-channel, staring at the sky, by French fishermen. He was buried at Beuzeval, near Trouville, in a Protestant cemetery, shortly afterwards.

* * *

John 'Rob Roy' MacGregor, probably the best known of our pioneers, was born at Gravesend on 24 January 1825, the son of Major Duncan MacGregor of the 31st Regiment of Foot (later the East Surreys). and the former Miss Elizabeth Dick. He did well to reach adulthood, surviving a number of encounters with the sea in his youth, two of them in his first year of life.

The family sailed for India, to where his father had been posted, in the East Indiaman *Kent*, 350 tons burden, which caught fire in a south-westerly gale in the Bay of Biscay on 1 March 1825. They were rescued by the brig *Cambria* in the nick of time. An eventful start in life, which was followed three or four months later by an infantile illness, his mother writing to a friend that he was reduced to one third of his previous size. The sea had not finished with the infant: his father was called to be near Horse

Guards in London and the family once again took ship, this time in Edinburgh aboard a steamer bound for London. Within twelve hours a hurricane was raging, the vessel lost her anchors and was drifting on to the Newcombe Sand off Great Yarmouth. The sea broke over the deck, nearly extinguishing the boilers as the vessel drifted towards speedy destruction. Then the gale suddenly fell, the wind veered completely round and the rest of the journey was accomplished in safety; his mother wrote 'poor little John has again been preserved in great danger'.

In 1834, when he was nine years old, the 93rd Highlanders, under the command of his father, were stationed at Canterbury, and there John went to his first school—The King's School within the precincts of the Cathedral. At the age of twelve, as he watched a ship in distress during a terrific storm, the lifeboat was launched and John jumped in to assist. At fifteen he had another encounter with the sea when he was wrecked in an iron boat outside Kingstown Harbour (now Dún Laoghaire), near Dublin, another narrow escape.

He studied at Cambridge, leaving in 1846 and moving to London to read for the Bar. Another protestant of strong conviction, he always observed the Sabbath and engaged in much philanthropic work, contributing substantial sums of money raised from his writing and lecturing, to a number of charities, including the Ragged Schools for the poor, some of which he helped to set up himself.

The cruise in the Yawl *Rob Roy* came about after his first two pioneering canoe voyages in 1865 and 1866; the books describing them had become best sellers, and he founded the Canoe Club. His exploits became known to the Emperor Napoleon III, who arranged for a boat exhibition to be held in Paris in 1867. In order to attend in style MacGregor sailed single-handed from London. To achieve this he commissioned a new 21ft. yawl, needing a larger boat to carry protestant literature, to distribute amongst what he considered to be the benighted catholics of France, afterwards writing another best selling account of the voyage.

In 1873, at 48, he became engaged and married, much to the surprise of his friends. His life continued with religious and philanthropic work. He loved children and his wife gave birth to a daughter in October 1875, a second daughter being born in 1882. He was a devoted husband, father and family man, although his preaching and lecturing took most of his time, with very little change until 1888 when he fell ill. He never recovered from this and died four years later on 16 July 1892. More than any other person MacGregor inspired affordable boating by a generation of small boat sailors in Britain and further afield.

* * *

The third of our early pioneers, the Hon. James Gordon, is considerably less well known today than the other three; in fact much of what we know about him has only recently come to light. Born the second son of the Earl of Aberdeen at the Ranger's house in Greenwich Park in 1845, he was a delicate child and suffered more than once from life-threatening illness in his first few years. By degrees however he acquired greater strength, becoming athletic with a reputation for daring, whilst remaining shy and undemonstrative. Educated initially at Cheam and later St. Andrews he entered Cambridge in 1865, and obtained a rowing blue in 1867. A notable scholar and a devout Christian, he taught at a local Sunday school and was held in exceptionally high regard by all who knew him.

Gordon's boat was probably built in the spring of 1867 by Searle of Lambeth, presumably on the lines of MacGregor's first boat as she looks very similar in hull form. Mention is made of 'new alterations and improvements' being 'carried out in a satisfactory manner', which explain the differences between the two. Surviving in remarkable condition to this very day, she is 14ft. long with a 26in. beam and a depth just under a foot. She has a cambered deck of cedar and was fitted with a wooden cutwater at the bow to 'divide the waves and give great buoyancy to the canoe'. Most importantly she was fitted with a drop keel to permit her to sail closer to the wind, the first known example of its use in a sailing canoe and possibly the earliest example on a British boat of any kind.

As far as we know the drop keel, then basically an elongated dagger board, was invented by a Royal Navy officer, Captain Shank, sometime before 1771, on a boat built in Boston, Massachusetts for Earl Percy, later Duke of Northumberland. In 1809

'Ροθιον', 1867 *('Rothion', or 'Surf' in English)*
Redrawn from a survey drawing by Graham Mackereth & Duncan Winning OBE, with a conjectural sail plan added.

another Royal Navy man, a Captain Schuldham, improved the earlier design by means of a pivot, which at the time was termed a revolving keel, and is now known as a centreboard or centreplate depending on the material used in its construction. The earliest example known to the author of a centre board boat of either type in the UK is in the early 1870s.

Gordon's boat was named *POΘION*, which translates from Greek as 'a wave dashing on the beach, a breaking wave, surf or surge'—*SURF* perhaps. In lower case it would be written as *ροθιον*. In upper case many Greek letters are identical in appearance to our Latin alphabet, though not always pronounced in the same way. The first letter 'P' is 'rho' and the transcription into the Roman alphabet is 'ROTHION'.

She had a small pivoting board, most likely sheet metal, with pulleys to raise and lower it within the case. She was also described with 'an unusually large mast and sail' so we can assume they were larger than that of the first Rob Roy canoe. She had a single lug sail which was used as a makeshift tent. The small cockpit and waterproof apron, and the cutwater, define her sea going potential, in contrast to previous canoes which were designed for inland waters.

Gordon was no doubt inspired by his elder brother's experiences on MacGregor's first cruise in his own canoe, which also survives, and he planned an extended cruise to the Mediterranean and back via Austria and the Rhine to Rotterdam, after first crossing the English Channel from St. Leonards to Boulogne. (He and his brother had also completed a Channel crossing from St. Leonards to Boulogne in what is described as 'an open boat' the previous year, nearly losing their lives in the process.)

The crossing is the first seagoing voyage ever recorded in a canoe; it epitomises the courage and determination shown by early leisure boaters, and given his tiny craft it was no mean achievement. It began on the 29 July; Gordon, having arrived at Dover with his newly built boat two days before, set off shortly after 9am. Once clear of the shelter of the cliffs the wind got up and the sail was lowered and reefed. Although the going was easier now another increase in wind made Gordon consider it prudent to return, and he made landfall somewhere between Dover and Deal. The boat was drawn up and a change of clothes and some food were followed by a cut-out being

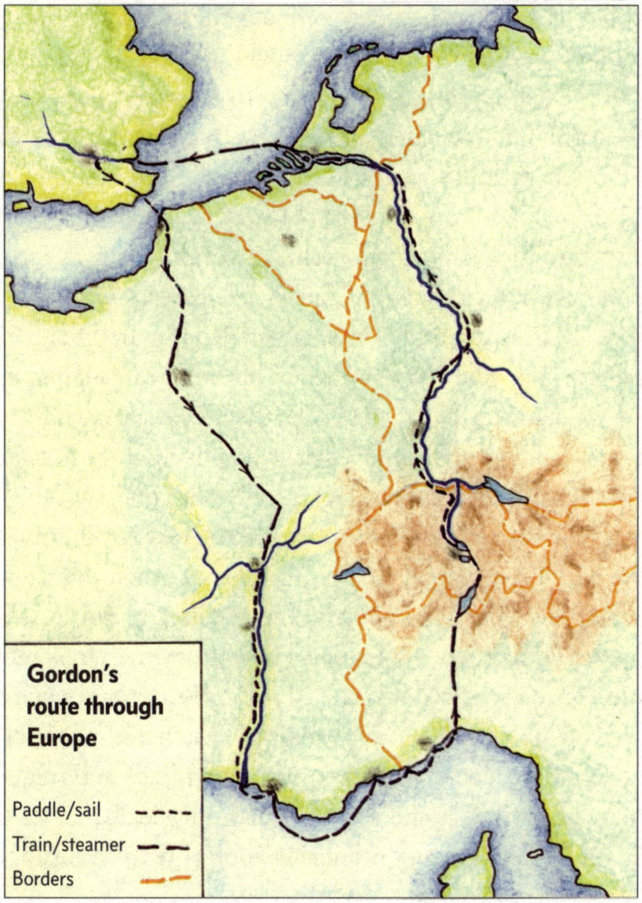

made in the floorboards for a sponge to keep the boat dry. By five o'clock the wind had dropped and *Rothion* was re-launched, and this time Gordon was confident of success. He paddled the boat out about a mile and set sail, but the wind dropped to nothing and he resumed paddling. A little later the wind changed direction and as darkness closed in the wind rose and waves began to hiss, foam and break around him; he was cold, wet and hungry.

Fear took hold as he saw the lights of a steamer bearing down upon him. He dropped the sail and paddled furiously, narrowly missing it, the port paddle wheel drenching him to the skin. Soon the sky began to clear and the Cap Gris Nez light appeared, the flash difficult to see in the heavy sea. By about 2 am the wind moderated and euphoria followed with the surges of the canoe in the breeze. Cold and fatigue now set in and Gordon fell asleep, a couple of times awaking with a start.

The tide then turned in a more favourable direction and with the dawn the coast of France came into view; an impulse to land at the nearest point was discarded, once the sound of waves beating upon the shore persuaded him to pursue his original plan and sail for Boulogne. The tide was now favourable but it carried him past the town to a small bay where he made landfall, and though the breakers gave him another drenching, he made a safe landing upon the beach. After hauling up *Rothion* he went to a small inn, changed his wet clothes and slept heavily until midday.

Gordon then took the train to Paris to view the Great Exhibition, and then on to Mâcon where he began the second part of his journey down the Saône to Lyon and then the Rhône all the way to Marseille and the Mediterranean. A steamer took him to Nice where he set off for Genoa by canoe. His journey then took him through Italy and Austria, into Germany and down the Rhine to Rotterdam where he embarked on a steamer, arriving home in Scotland, weather-beaten and worn on 11 September, having survived surging inclement weather, torrents, rapids and frequent immersion in the water. Alas, he arrived home a broken man physically, and a tragic shooting accident in early 1868 brought a very promising young life to an abrupt end.

* * *

The last of our four, Empson Edward Middleton was born in 1838, the son of Boswell Middleton, Advocate-General in Jamaica, who died when Empson was 15. His paternal grandfather was Empson Middleton of Ebberston Hall, Yorkshire, a very wealthy man, and his maternal grandfather a Master of Trinity House, who had connections with King William IV and was apparently held in some personal esteem by the Monarch. Before his death his father had applied for a commission

KATE, 1869
Built by Forrestt of Limehouse;
3.75 Tons BM; LOA 23ft; LWL 21ft; beam 7ft; draught 3ft. 9in.
Ballast 21 cwt and sail area about 208 sq. ft.

in the Navy for the young Empson, but as he was a month or two over the age of 14 this was declined. There were ship owners on both sides of the family and when his father died, much to his indignation, he was packed off to sea as a junior officer and sailed to Australia on a square rigger, the *Albemarle* owned by his cousin a Mr Tindal, but the Mercantile Marine did not suit him and he obtained a 'quittance' on his return two years later.

Inspired by the Indian Mutiny, he joined the 51st Light Infantry regiment (later the King's Own Yorkshire Light Infantry) as an Ensign in 1858, and served in the Punjab until 1864. Unfortunately, in 1859, when he purchased a commission as Lieutenant, due to maladministration by the Regimental Paymaster he was cheated out of 15 months' pay, some £100, and although a very wealthy man was so indignant that he sold out at the first opportunity. Middleton's privileged background had given him a very high opinion of himself, and these difficult early years probably did little to improve his character and may have contributed to the extreme eccentricity and obsessive behaviour that was the hallmark of the later years of his life. He died a resentful man in 1916.

His ground breaking cruise in 1869 was a triumph of obstinacy, endurance and determination, in the face of atrocious weather conditions. It was done at a time when equipment and facilities were virtually non-existent; his account is a fitting testimony to a brave, if foolhardy, man. He was indeed fortunate to survive the ordeal though, unsurprisingly, he does not appear to share this view in his eminently readable account of the adventure. It all came about after Middleton read MacGregor's *The Voyage Alone in The Yawl Rob Roy* and, suitably inspired, he decided to go one better.

He completed a circumnavigation of England, in the hope of attracting similar public acclaim to MacGregor's before him. He achieved this to a degree, but his fame was short lived and faded away after the publication of the cruise account.

He was not an experienced small boat sailor but had some two years' full time sea-going experience and a good reputation as a helmsman, from his service on the *Albemarle*. He also hired a small cutter and made a dozen or so trips during the very

severe winter of 1868 whilst the *Kate* was in build, to gain experience of the type. The *Kate* was built in early 1869 by Messrs. Forrestt of Limehouse, who also built the yawl *Rob Roy* for Macgregor. The lines were drawn by a John White of West Cowes, for a vessel similar to *Rob Roy* but with one or two alterations, including a heavier iron keel. Middleton also modified the sail plan, following his experiences with the cutter. She certainly seems to have given a good account of herself and Middleton was full of praise for her.

I know of a couple of engravings of *Kate*, along with fairly detailed written description of her, but there is little else that I have been able to track down by way of drawings at the time of writing. The engravings do vary somewhat in detail, by way of artist's licence. What I have tried to do is to build up from their information and produce a more detailed specification, along with approximations as to form, displacement and sail plan in order to have a glimpse into what she might have been like.

Kate's cruise began on the evening of 15 July at Limehouse after a few modifications had been completed following her launch on the 10th. The journey was made all the more remarkable by Middleton dining and sleeping ashore virtually every night, which flew in the face of the accepted wisdom to stay in deep water and not attempt to approach land in foul weather. He was governed by the tides, rowing for long and arduous periods to catch a favourable flood or ebb. It is perhaps as well he did dine ashore, as his sea-going diet, apart from the odd biscuit, appears to consist for the most part of raw eggs washed down with a half pint of sherry. He completed the trip on the 23rd of September, after 62 gruelling days.

* * *

By the later nineteenth century leisure boating was an idea whose time had come, given the luxury of spare time, and the sufficient income on which to enjoy it which resulted, for many, from the Industrial Revolution. These were four of those in its vanguard, who by their ambitious exploits and popular accounts of them inspired a generation to establish the pursuit we enjoy today.

2 Working boat conversions

IN THE LATE 19TH CENTURY most boats were working craft, evolved over centuries to suit a specific purpose, generally fishing or cargo carrying, and adapted to suit local conditions. Double-ended hulls were fairly common in the British Isles, local types including Yoals in Shetland and Lincolnshire (Yolls), Skiffs in Scotland, Mule Cobles in the North East, Crabbers in Norfolk and Peter Boats on the Thames. Most were built heavily, to withstand the rigours of their use, and cheaply. The British working craft is a fundamental part of our rich and diverse maritime heritage, much undervalued and often neglected; I can do no better than quote Conor O'Brien:

> "These boats... were built by poor men for poor men, suffering from the two great spiritual evils of poverty—ignorance and prejudice. That they still produced fine boats is to the glory of natural man, who, living close to elemental things, develops an instinct for the earth or the sea which passes sophisticated understanding.

The two-masted rig was popular amongst working craft for a number of reasons, and was often found in boats as small as 14ft. This is because individual sails are smaller than with a single mast, so easier to handle both in a blow and in the confines of a harbour. It also offers a variety of sail configurations to suit prevailing conditions, with a basic set of sail sizes it reduced the need for reefing whilst at work, a suitable choice being selected and rigged to suit before setting sail. And with a mizzen alone set, a boat can be held head to wind when working nets, lines or pots. Importantly, especially in the smaller boats, the centre of effort of the sail plan is lower than that of a single-masted rig, reducing the heeling moment and making the boat less tender in a breeze.

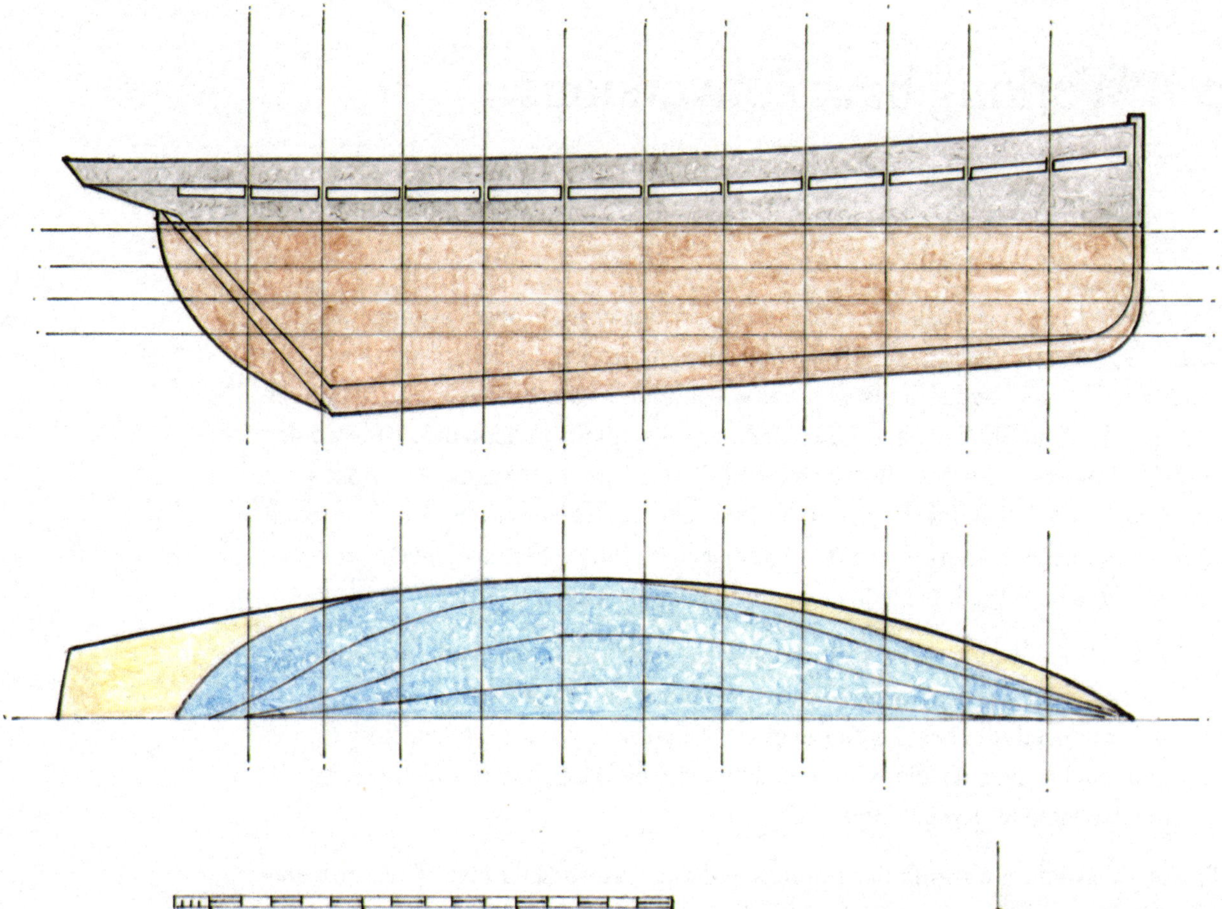

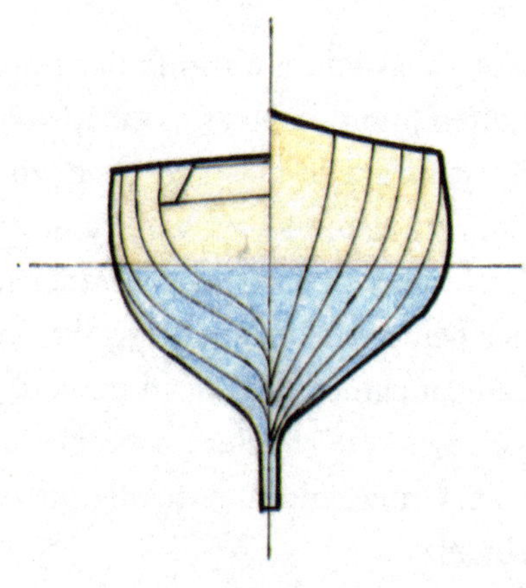

MOSQUITO, 1848

A steel cutter built by Mare's Shipyard
at Blackwall on the Thames.
59ft. LWL with a 15ft. 4in. Beam, draught about 12 feet.

The design of craft specifically for leisure began towards the end of the 18th century; but 'design' is probably an overstatement for what was merely the adaptation of existing hull forms, and modification to sail plans. One of the earliest attempts to understand the hydrodynamics of hull design was by Frederick H. Chapman (1725-1802), an eminent naval architect born in Sweden of English parents, whose *Architectura Navalis Mercatoria* of 1768 became the definitive work on ship design. He was the first to draw attention to the importance of finer ends on the underwater hull, and for the first time devised mathematical theories for the design of ships—in particular relating to displacement and stability—some of which are still in use today.

In the mid-19th century the British naval architect J. Scott Russell (1808-1882) expanded upon this earlier work by Chapman and published new research on the relationship between hull and waves, known as the 'wave line theory', which was adopted by many designers of the time. This led directly to the development of finer ends on the underwater hull shape and heralded a significant shift in opinion on the design of ships. Russell designed and built a 60ft. boat *Wave* on this principle, and others were to follow. The most pivotal of these was the steel cutter *Mosquito* of 1848, 59ft. on the waterline, designed by Thomas Waterman and built at Blackwall on the Thames by Mare's shipyard.

Mosquito defied the prejudice of her time towards the 'long lean bow', she failed to sink as prophesied, and had a long and successful career, finishing up at Barrow-in-Furness as a pilot boat until the turn of the century. That she did not achieve recognition for the groundbreaking design that she was, and that it was left to others to develop her principles further, was unfortunate; but original thinking had infiltrated the design process, which now began with a blank sheet and an open mind.

The Institution of Naval Architects, later to be granted the prefix 'Royal', was formed on 16 January 1860, and three of the founders were John MacGregor, J. Scott Russell and John White, who had designed *Kate* for Middleton. Design knowledge gradually increased, resulting in the design process becoming much more detailed and the end product more predictable. With much improved levels of communication the science of naval architecture began to flourish.

The next boat in our story is *Dauntless*; she was a converted Thames 'Peter boat' built in 1836, and converted in 1872 by a man called Albert Strange. The type had its origins in the Anglo-Saxon era, the name first appearing in the 14th century and is reputedly derived from St. Peter, the fisherman. Peter boats were fairly numerous on the Thames from Windsor downstream into London, where they were smaller rowing craft. Below London Bridge in the Port of London the larger sailing versions plied their trade down to the tidal Estuary and also in the rivers of Essex as far up as the Stour and down to the Medway in the south. The rig changed over the years, but both sprit and dipping lug were represented.

The original which I have redrawn is the only known lines plan of the type, although there are a number of engravings, notably those beautifully detailed and evocative studies by E. W. Cooke. Alas no original examples of the type survive as far as is known, but very recently two replicas were built for the film *Robin Hood*. These were 18 and 22 feet long, built by Mark Edwards at Richmond Boathouses, the decks and planking in sweet chestnut, copper fastened, with stringers, knees, gunwale, etc. of oak. Interestingly, sweet chestnut was much favoured by boatbuilders of old who were on piecework, as it was much easier to work than the specified oak. The practice was a bit underhand, hence most boats were wrongly described as being built of oak.

Here is the legend behind the name as I know it, though I cannot of course vouch for its authenticity:

> "When Edward the Confessor builded his great Church to the glory of God and the honour of the blessed Saint Peter, where Henry's proud Abbey of Westminster now stands, it is recounted that upon the eve of the consecration, a solitary fisherman was hauling his nets from his boat upon the shallows of the wide river. A venerable looking traveller hailed him from the shore and asked that he might be ferried across to the new Abbey Church upon the isle of Thorney, and forthwith as the stranger landed the great windows of the church were filled with light, and the lofty stone vaulting with the glorious music of the Hosts of Heaven. And thus was the church that

DAUNTLESS, 1872

Redrawn from the original drawing. 18ft. LOA with a 6ft. beam and a draught of about 1ft. 8in.
The false keel and filler pieces at the ends can be clearly seen.
The steel plate fixed to the bottom of the false keel would have added about 1 cwt of ballast.

> night consecrated by the heavenly choirs and the holy Saint Peter himself. No coin did the saint leave on the after thwart of the poor fisherman's little boat, but a blessing to all good Thames fishermen, which has lasted down to our own times—until the days when Satan, as some do aver, placed steam-boats to ply upon the river, and stone embankments along its shallows, and turned it into little better than a tidal mill-sluice.

This is the first authentic record we have of the little 'Peter' boat, which was a characteristic Thames type for longer than the present Abbey walls have stood. The grateful fisherman after that long-remembered night evidently took the liberty of calling his boat after the fisherman's Saint who had so honoured his humble craft.

The following is an amusing account of an incident on the Thames around 1870 told some time later and relates to how Albert Strange came to acquire the *Dauntless*. It gives us a nice snapshot of a time in history when leisure sailing was in its infancy and working boats were the order of the day. 'Shrimptown' refers to Gravesend, on the south shore of the lower Thames in Kent, and *Eliza Jane* was of a fishing type known as a Bawley, a transom sterned cutter with a loose footed gaff mainsail, equipped to boil the shrimp catch on the way back to market; LO refers to London as the port of registry.

> "One Saturday afternoon, a good many years ago, the *Eliza Jane* LO 91 was brought up off Shrimptown, Bob, the Skipper, was, as he expressed it, 'bilin' the results of the previous night's catch, which amounted to some bushels of first class shrimps. It was a pleasant afternoon, and a smart WSW breeze was crisping and curling the young flood and making the old *Eliza Jane* sheer about a good deal, as the Skipper ladled net after net-full of brown shrimps from out the copper, which they had a moment before entered—a pale translucent skipping mass—and spread them all hot and smoking out on the stern sheets to cool. Lolling on the big jib, which had been taken off the bow-sprit, but not stowed away, was a lad—a lumpish, half sailor boy half

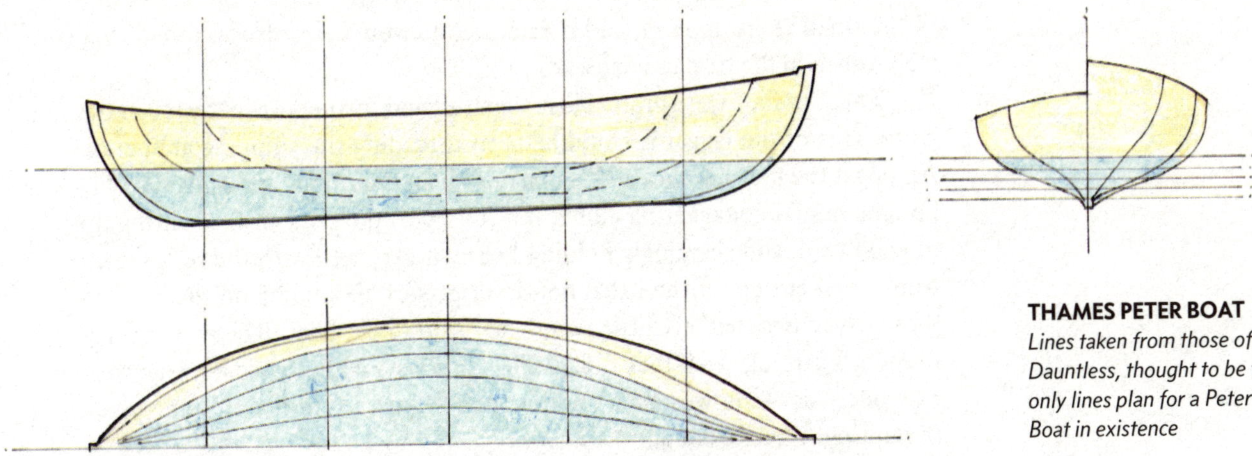

THAMES PETER BOAT
Lines taken from those of Dauntless, thought to be the only lines plan for a Peter Boat in existence

school boy sort of customer, reading aloud from a well thumbed copy of the *Comic History of England*, Bob paying the deepest attention to the recital, but with the watchfulness instinctive to a fisherman, constantly casting an eye up and down the river.

For an ignorant man, and in one sense he was ignorant, as he could barely read or write, Bob was the most eager searcher after knowledge imaginable, and the lad who was reading to him had many and many a night before, when fishing along the 'edge of the sand', found himself puzzled to answer the enormous and endless number of questions on all subjects under the sun, that Bob would ask him and, such as the boy's small stock of knowledge was, it was incessantly raked up and over, like a well trawled ground, in the endeavour to quench Robert's unquenchable thirst for information.

It is possible that Bob didn't see all the jokes, and that History in a comic dress would be slightly misleading as useful knowledge; but the account of Henry the Eighth's various trials in the matrimonial line was being followed with deep interest, and the shrimps steadily changed colour and filled up the roomy stern more and more, the breeze as steadily freshened. Suddenly the reading was interrupted by Bob's remarking: 'Here's the Yots comin!

my eye, ain't they a givin it to 'em!' It was a Saturday afternoon race of one of the small clubs up river, and they certainly were being driven for all they were worth in the turn to windward.

Three or four were pretty close together and further down the reach the white sails of the laggards could be seen threading the shipping at anchor. Amongst the first few was a small boat with an enormous spritsail and a big jib on a bumkin, staggering along, rap full, with the crew of four sitting up to windward, and seemingly holding her own very well with the rest, which were small cutters of the usual nondescript sort abounding on the river in those days. 'See that 'ere little peterboat,' said Bob. 'They'll blow 'er over if they ain't careful, see if they don't. She was Dusty Miller's old boat, an wer-ry tender too—she was allus middlin' fast—Dusty sold her to some gents this spring, when 'e bought the *Fiddle*.

It certainly looked as if Bob's prophetic utterance would be fulfilled, as the boat stood on towards us, heeling frightfully in the puffs which slammed out from between the houses, but as yet keeping right side up. 'E's come fur enough out o' the tide,' said Bob, when suddenly the boat stayed, and before she was well on the other tack was headed by a foul puff, and almost stood still. Then before one could wink almost, down came another puff, and over she went, slap, and sunk straightway. Bob sprang aft, pulled up the skiff that was hanging astern, tumbled in and was pulling toward the swimming crew in an instant. 'Give 'er a 'ard sheer out !' he yelled as he departed, 'one on 'ems drivin' wery near aboard ye. Chuck 'im a line as 'e comes by!' All this took but an instant, and hardly had the boat sheered than the man was driv-ing almost within a yard of her. The boy threw him the end of the main sheet, and pulled him alongside, but could not lift him aboard, so he had to hang on a bit until Bob arrived with three others, two in the skiff and one tow-ing astern. When they had all got on board they presented a sorry sight, and doubtless felt as uncomfortable as they looked.

'Well' said Bob, 'yer boat's gone, watch'yer going to do next?' One of them, probably the owner, said 'I'm very much obliged to you for picking us up, but as most of my money was in my coat pocket, I can't offer vou anything, just now, but if you'll—Bob interrupted him here, 'I don't want nothing fer pickin' on yer up, but watch'yer going to do about the boat? She'll have to be cocked up too else the Thames Conservatives'll be arter yer.' Bob meant Conservancy, no doubt, but he always insisted on calling them Conservatives. 'Oh, well,' said the owner, 'if you like to take her for the trouble of getting her up, you may, I've had enough of her'. 'Werry well,' said Bob, I'll heave 'er up, and if yer changes yer mind, and pays me for the trouble, yer knows where to find 'er, when she's afloat again. I'd better shove yer ashore now, I expects yer ain't werry warm.

So saying, Bob hauled the skiff alongside again and they got aboard. As they shoved off towards the causeway the one that had been helped by the main sheet extracted with difficulty a half-crown from his wet pocket and threw it to the boy, who smilingly laid it down on the cabin top. When Bob returned with the skiff he meditativelv took a fresh quid*, and went on with his boiling, saying, 'Well, go on, let's 'ave some more about 'that 'ere 'Enery the Heighth 'e was a masterpiece 'e wos'. But the boy was rather too much excited by the recent rescue to read, and drew Robert's attention to the half-crown, which he pocketed, saying, 'Werry decent lot o' gents, but I reckon they won't want to go yot racin' jest yet awhile. We'll get 'er up at low water, an' see wot she's like.'

Sure enough she was got up that next low water, and bailed out with a bucket. The boy stayed to watch the operation, and it was broad daylight on Sunday morning when she was rowed ashore, none the worse for her sojourn on the bottom. As Bob proceeded to moor her, he remarked: 'Now, she's the werry thing fer you to go padhoofin up an' down Sea Reach in, ain't she? Jest the werry packet as 'ud soot yer down to the round.' The boy's eyes glistened at the bare idea of owning a boat, but he didn't think he could afford to buy her, and he was sure his father wouldn't hear of such a thing.

'Well, I'll tell yer wot I'll do,' said the faithful Robert, 'If them 'ere gent doesn't turn up an' claim her, I'll cut the sails down ter reasonable size, and

---

* A wad of chewing tobacco.

> will fit 'er out fer a yot fer yer, an' you can pay me when you gits the money. It won't be much ennyway.' And, as the 'gents' never turned up from that day to this, she was fitted out again for a 'yot' and that is how the, *Dauntless* came into my possession. Before the transaction was completed we were sitting in her one afternoon, and Bob was preparing a fresh quid when gazing absently at her name-board which was screwed just inside the aftercoaming with *Psyche* in gilt letters on it, he remarked, 'I reckon them gents wasn't werry first class scholors, I never seed "fish" spelt like that afore!'

The use of fishing boats was the earliest development in Corinthian* recreational sailing. Conversions remained a part of the yachting scene for many years, with some examples still sailing today. Double-ended ships' lifeboats were readily available at modest cost, and in spite of the hull form being somewhat unsuitable for a sailing boat, many were converted with varying degrees of success, quite often to the scorn of yacht designers.

The best of the lifeboat conversions was probably the like of *Dulcibella* which was an RNLI pulling and sailing lifeboat built in 1880 and converted around 1896; she featured in Erskine Childers' novel *The Riddle of the Sands*. Formerly *Vixen* and re-named after his sister, she was converted by Joseph Price of Margate, who was a lifeboat conversion specialist. She was originally the 28ft × 7ft 9in lifeboat *Thomas Chapman*. This type of boat was lightly constructed with double-diagonal planking coupled with a pronounced sheer and very low freeboard amidships for rowing.

The conversion consisted of removing the fore and aft cuddies and belting, adding new carvel planking doubled over the hull from the waterline up, raising the sheer and forming a false counter stern to extend the overall length by some 3ft. A gaff yawl rig, new deck, bulwarks, cockpit and cabin completed it. The drawing is representative of the type, and not specifically of the original boat or the larger 35ft version used in the film. The conversion is surprisingly pleasing to the eye, albeit that the sailing performance would be limited, as with all lifeboat hulls, even with a centreplate fitted.

---

* Amateur, without paid hands.

LIFEBOAT CONVERSION c1895

Showing the carvel planking overlaid on the double diagonal planking of the lifeboat; she would have needed a considerable amount of ballast to achieve the required waterline, perhaps several tons of iron pigs.

3 Emergence of the Canoe Yawl

The Canoe Club was formed in July 1866 and held its first Regatta at Hampton Court in April 1887. John 'Rob Roy' MacGregor was the first Captain and HRH the Prince of Wales the first Commodore. Within a year it boasted over 100 members and a 20-strong branch was formed at Cambridge, with a Mr J. B. Hopwood as Captain; in 1873 it received a Royal Warrant and became the Royal Canoe Club. The club expanded, with an Eastern Branch on the Humber and a Northern on the Mersey and other independent clubs were formed, including the Cruising Club, the Clyde, Bradford, Forth, Carlow, Trent Wanderers and Castle Troy Canoe Clubs.

The early cruising and racing canoes were mostly of the 'Rob Roy' type, with two derivatives, namely the 'Nautilus' and 'Pearl' series. There were three boats built with the name *Rob Roy*: the original canoe was built in 1865, a detailed description of which appeared in the *Transactions* of the Institution of Naval Architects, and another in 1866, which was an improved version, based on MacGregor's experiences on his first cruise and again well described, this time in his second book *Rob Roy on the Baltic* published in 1867. This became the basis of most of the later canoe designs, and is one of the earliest purpose-designed leisure craft. Her successor, the third version which had cruised the River Jordan, survives to this day as part of the National Small Boat Collection, held by the National Maritime Museum Cornwall, in Falmouth.

'A canoe ought to fit a man like a coat; and to secure this the measure of the man should be taken for his canoe' according to MacGregor, so she was designed 'to be used by a man 6 feet high, 12 stone, and with boots one foot long in the sole. At 14ft. overall, a 26in. beam, with a main and jib in total 19½ square feet of sail, she was built of oak with a mahogany 'streak' (sheer strake) and cedar decks. The mast was tapered and the spars were bamboo. She weighed 71lbs. complete with fittings.

'Nautilus' was the name given to a series of canoes designed by Warrington Baden-Powell, a very keen sailor and the solicitor brother of the founder of the Scouting movement. The size varied with purpose, for example fourteen feet overall with a 33in. beam for sailing and sleeping aboard or fifteen feet overall with a 30in. beam for sailing and paddling. The rig, now lug yawl, was larger, a little over 50 square feet in total for the cruising versions although the racers carried much more, around 110 square feet. Later much larger versions were designed including, in 1893, one of twenty feet overall with a five-foot beam and 'considerable depth' described as a 'splendid cruising yawl'.

The 'Pearl' canoes were a range of seven designs by E. B. Tredwen, a Cornishman who, in 1868 and aged sixteen, came to live in London. He was another notable sailor of the time who also came to be known for his 'Barge Yachts' which were small cruisers based on the flat-bottomed Thames barges, of which we shall hear more later. These canoes were fairly similar to the 'Nautilus' series, and also came in cruising and racing versions, except that Tredwen generally favoured a flat, rather than a rising floor, on the basis that the canoeist could sit lower, and further to windward, when heeled.

Although other canoe clubs did exist there is little information as to whether they developed their own local types. Only the Eastern Branch (later to become The Humber Yawl Club which formed in 1883) and the Northern Branch (later the Mersey Canoe Club) which became independent of the RCC in 1873 after a dispute over subscriptions, developed their own individual and distinctive designs. To a lesser extent both the Clyde and Tyne Canoe Clubs developed specific 'Clyde' and 'Wear' canoes; purists may argue, but they were very similar to other sailing and paddling versions of the type.

The Clyde canoe was perhaps more notable; one, the *Lark* (1878) later *Wren* described in *The Field* as 'a cross between a birch bark and a kayak', had hollow lines and fine ends, 'perhaps too fine to accord with an English canoeist's idea of a cruising canoe, and are indeed finer than the ends of many Clyde canoes'. She was 14ft. 6in. x 2ft. 6in., of teak and white pine with mahogany decks. The type was quite popular within the Clyde Canoe Club, which had a very active cruising section during the 1870s and 1880s.

NAUTILUS No. 5, 1879

by W Baden-Powell. 14ft with a beam of 33in., she was probably the first canoe with a true keel. She carried 250 lb of lead ballast, a 65 lb centre plate, and drew about 15in. She won the 1879 RCC Championship Cup, beating the 1878 winner, a Pearl canoe.

The canoe yawl emerged as a boat for the middle classes, and both cruising and racing versions developed alongside each other. This evolution came from an amalgam of canoe and workboat types, the canoes becoming heavier for more extended cruising and the workboats lighter for ease of handling. The entrenched opinion of the early years, that five or six tons was about right for a 'single-hander', was repeatedly found wanting and early pioneers made extended voyages in much smaller and lighter craft. Similarly, on the racing scene the canoe yawls, forerunners of the modern ultra light racers, were sweeping the board against the traditional 0.5 Rater on the Solent and elsewhere, provoking heated argument and accusations of cheating, a perennial hazard in class racing.

As cruising and racing continued to develop towards the end of the 19th century, the designs started to achieve much higher levels of sophistication as their authors increased their knowledge of naval architecture and the relationship between design and performance. Boats were now designed as leisure craft in their own right, and whilst the well-to-do used professional designers and established yacht builders, the growing demand from the emerging middle class enabled a number of new, amateur designers to flourish, some achieving standards at least equal to the professionals. Very prolific, they made use of small boat builders experienced in producing working boats to offer an elegant and affordable alternative to the gentleman's yacht, on a smaller scale, of lighter construction, and incorporating considerable innovation in hull design and rig, the latter particularly among sailing canoes.

No better illustration of this is to be found than in the articulate and amusing correspondence columns of the contemporary yachting press. Contentious issues were frequently debated in heated but gentlemanly manner over long periods of time. Some publications, such as *The Yachtsman*, first published in April 1891, were weekly, yet were never short of lively and readable correspondence, especially in the early years. The quality of this correspondence started to decline after the First World War, and the effortless, instantaneous and generally anonymous online forum of today is unlikely to restore it.

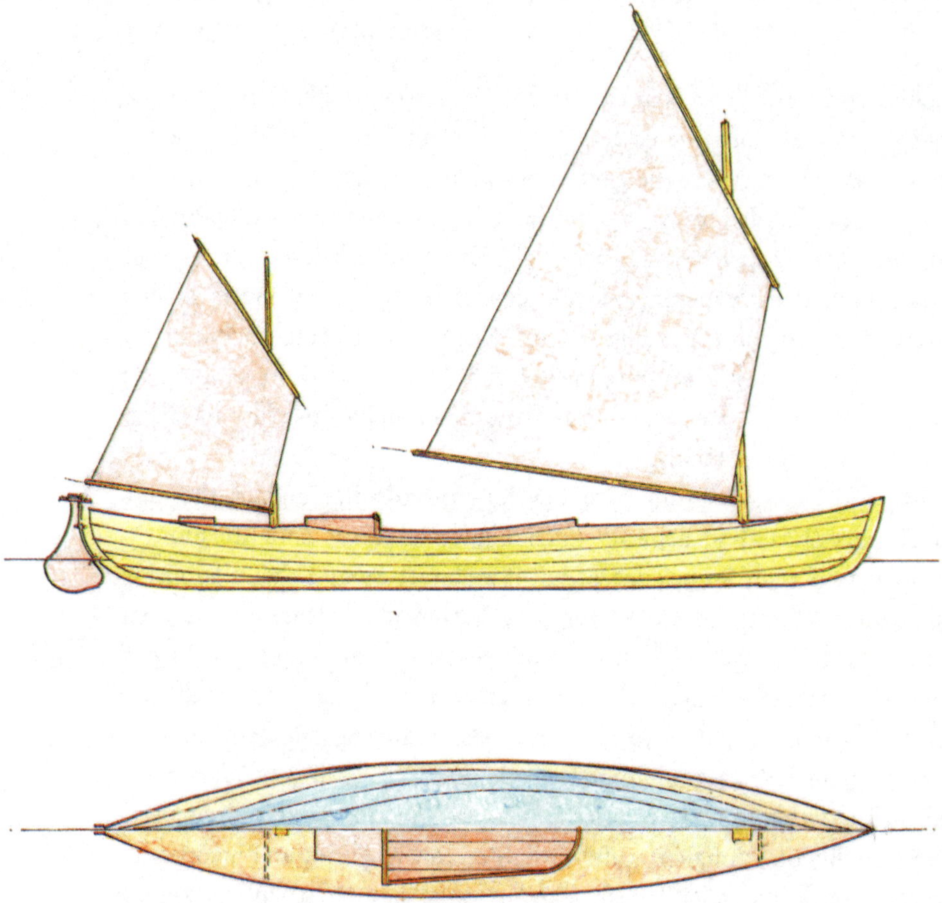

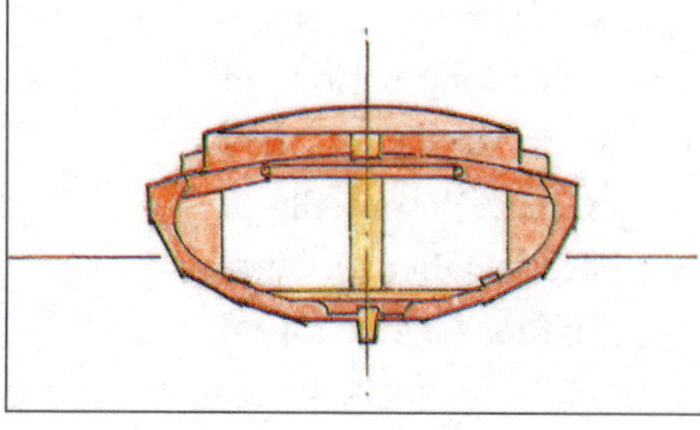

LARK, 1875

A Clyde Canoe designed by C G King, 14ft 6in x 29½in with a draught of 10in. The rig shown is for racing, a 36 sq. ft. main and 11 sq. ft. Mizzen. For cruising she carried just a 25 sq. ft. main. The hollow waterlines and pronounced sheer are features of this design.

The heavier canoe designs developed on the Mersey and Humber were a response to the rougher waters of these large estuaries than the earlier, finer sailing canoes could handle. There then began an evolution from canoes towards more of a working boat hull form, while working boats themselves became lighter and finer. The estuary canoe types became more seaworthy as more experience in cruising was accumulated, while the lightweight sailing canoes continued to evolve independently, and part company with this narrative.

Interest grew in heavier, more seaworthy types such as the Mersey Canoes which originated around 1877 and were built by Sam Bond of Birkenhead, of which the *Vital Spark*, *c*1880, is a notable example; she had a both a small ballast keel and internal ballast under the deck. Built to a very high specification of yellow pine planking on oak frames with a teak top strake, and lockers. The lockers were made to incorporate air bags or zinc boxes for buoyancy. This interest in heavier boats developed as the Eastern Canoe Club itself declined and the Humber Yawl Club was formed in 1883 with four former ECC members, including a young George Holmes.

To improve sea-keeping and sail-carrying ability it was necessary to breach the 2ft. 6in. maximum beam of the sailing canoe. George Holmes was one of the first designers to take this step. He was born in 1861 in Hornsea, a small coastal town in the East Riding of Yorkshire, his father owning a tannery business in nearby Hull.

George developed a keen interest in small craft of all kinds. His first boat was a 20ft version of a local type, the coble, a beach boat with a dipping lug rig, fine forefoot and deep rudder. However the need for something smaller and lighter that could be launched and retrieved more easily was uppermost in his mind. He entered into his father's business, now named Thos. Holmes & Son, in his early twenties and with his time now limited a more suitable craft became a necessity. In addition to the Humber estuary he also sailed on Hornsea Mere, which was sheltered, inland water with boats for hire. The Mere was also home to J. A. Akester, a small boatyard which was to build a number of Holmes's designs over the years.

Gerrie of 1881 was his first design; with a workmanlike lug yawl rig and with oars as a secondary means of propulsion, she was one of the earliest examples of the

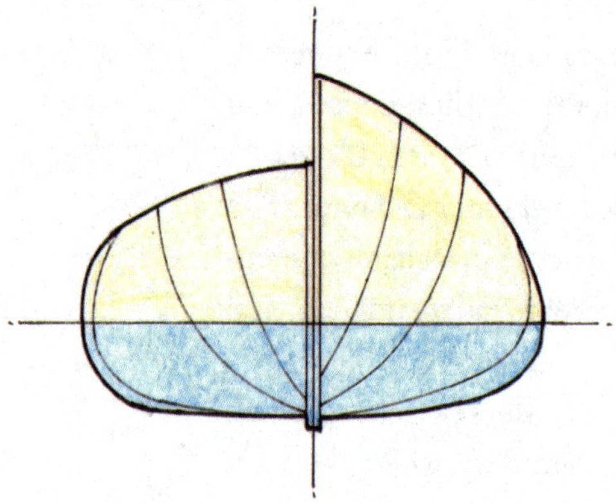

Wear canoe

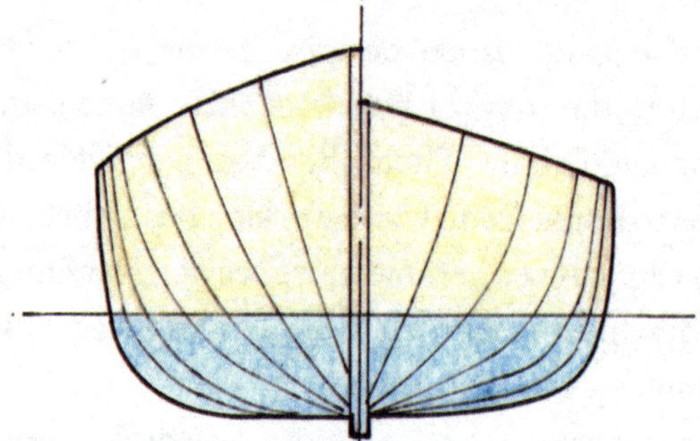

Nautilus No. 6

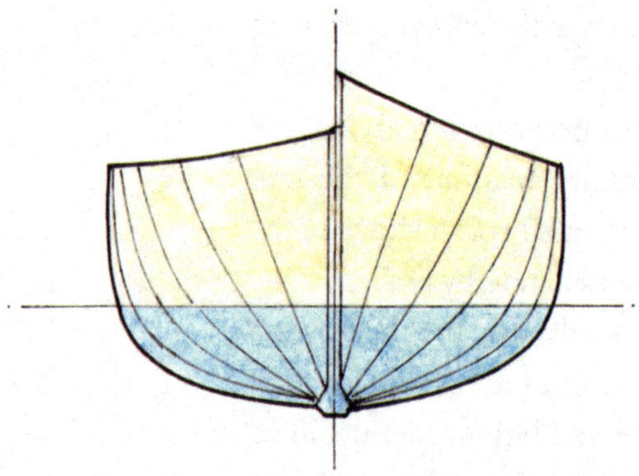

Pearl No. 5

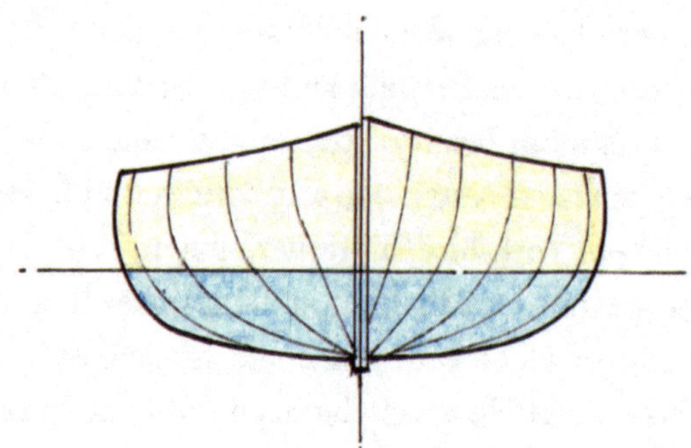

Rob Roy

CANOE HULL FORMS

—comparison showing Lines and Midsection of four local types. The Wear canoe is quite extreme but Nautilus No. 6 and Pearl No 5 are fairly similar and more typical of the emerging type, albeit the Nautilus has a much firmer bilge, whereas the Rob Roy is much more of the traditional Kayak hull form.

transition of beam away from the narrow paddling and sailing canoes. An otherwise innovative design, she had the cod's head and mackerel tail of an earlier outdated hull form, and without a keel or centreplate she was not a success.

His next design, the *Cassie* of 1883, was a much better boat, with firm bilges, smaller rig, a centre plate with a 3ft. 3in. beam; it became the definitive Humber canoe yawl of the time, and a number of examples were built. Holmes was a keen sailor and became a prolific small boat designer, commissioning a new boat nearly every year, continuously refining and adapting his designs after a season or so of sailing. He was one of the most innovative designers during the 1880s, and designed around 50 boats, of various types, during a long life which ended in 1940.

Boats were now being designed specifically for the Humber, one of them by Holmes's boyhood friend John Hamilton Jr. At 18ft the Humber Yawl *Viking* of 1886 owed her ancestry to the double-ended working boats, and though of the same dimensions as *Vital Spark* she was deeper with a centreplate, a most seaworthy boat which may survive to the present day—she was still sailing in the 1980s but her current whereabouts are unknown, in spite of considerable efforts to locate her. Hamilton is also credited as the first man to add a cabin to a Humber yawl in 1887.

Light displacement was now being promoted for cruising boats, in particular by Albert Strange. He was an experienced sailor; he began cruising around 1871, following the events which led to him acquiring his 'Yot' which have been described. He had long admired the little canoe yawls, particularly those of his friend George Holmes, thus when he started designing them he had almost twenty years of regular, mostly single-handed, cruising under his belt. His designs were based on sound practical experience and, coupled with his considerable artistic ability, soon established him as an amateur designer of some note; commissions came thick and fast.

Albert George Strange was born in Gravesend on 29 July 1855, the son of George l'Strange, a china and glass dealer, and Sarah Elizabeth, née Jarman, who was his second wife. His first wife Mary had died in childbirth in 1849, along with an infant Thomas, the twin of Charles, who survived, along with their first child, Elizabeth. Albert's mother died in 1874, aged thirty-five. His interest in boats started early in life

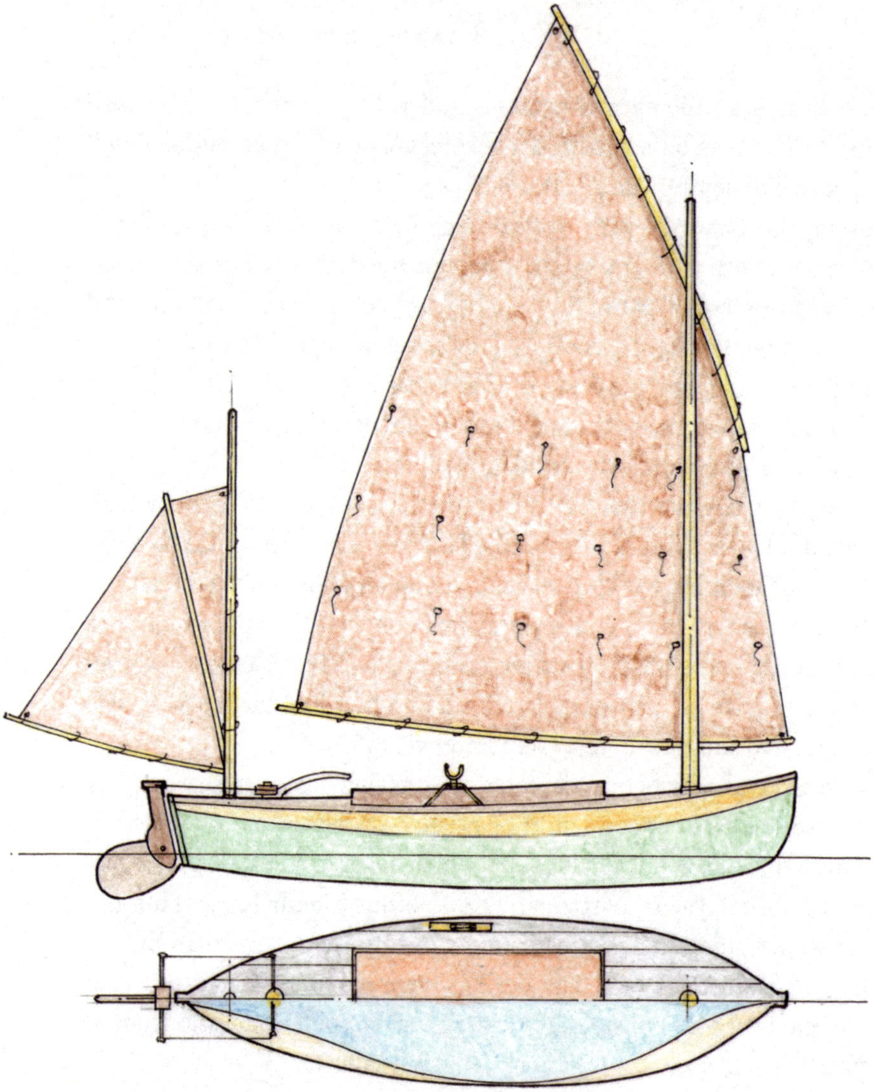

GERRIE, 1881

by George Holmes. 12ft 3in x 3ft 3½in, clinker built of yellow pine; an interesting Canoe Yawl design in several ways. She has a very shallow 2in keel but had a workmanlike rig and, unusually, the alternative propulsion is not paddles but oars in brass rowlocks. These, 'after several costly and unsuccessful experiments' were later replaced with iron outriggers. She has a hollow bow and a fine run aft which is quite advanced for the time, and although unsuccessful she was another step along the way.

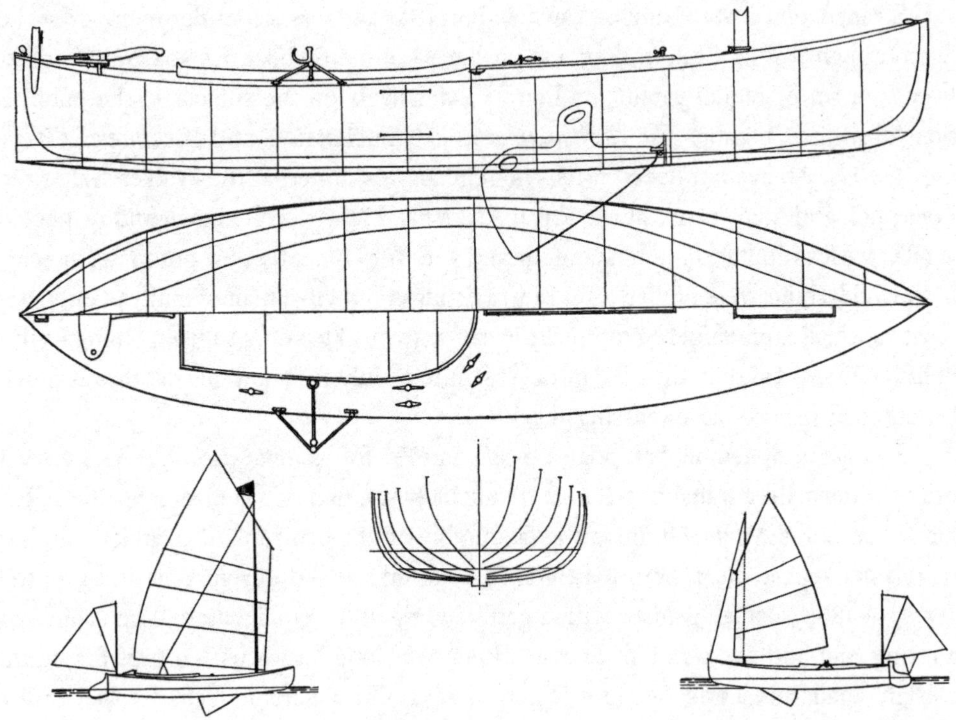

CASSIE, 1883

by George Holmes. 14ft x 3ft 4in; another imaginative design, she has a little more beam than was usual for the time and was a break from the RCC model. Her construction is not known but she carried 85 sq. ft. of sail for cruising, and for racing an extra-large mainsail took it up to 135 sq. ft. She had a 70 lb. iron centre board and was un-ballasted but when racing an extra 1 cwt. of gravel or sand in bags was added. Again the auxiliary propulsion was oars with outriggers, no doubt from Holmes' experiences with Gerrie. He also made the outriggers removable; his work at this time was one of continual development.

and when he was fourteen a church choir outing on a Thames fishing boat led to him being a regular 'hand' on fishing trips and accompanying his fisherman friend Bob, who acted as a pilot, on the local racing yachts, which he greatly enjoyed.

His father had in mind a career in the law for young Albert, but he persuaded his father to let him attend Slade School of Art in South Kensington, where he became a certificated Art Master, going on to the Liverpool College of Art. In 1881 he took up the post of Headmaster of the newly formed School of Art at Scarborough. Under his tutelage the school flourished and produced a number of extremely talented and subsequently well known artists. He married his childhood sweetheart Julia Louise Woolard, a Quaker, after his appointment, and she bore him two sons, George and Albert, and a daughter Dorothy who died early aged twenty-eight.

Strange joined the Humber Yawl Club in 1891 and was a founder member of the Scarborough Sailing Club in 1895. He produced some 160 boat designs and a further twenty or so for model yachts, and wrote extensively on the subject in the publications of the day, notably *The Yachtsman*, a weekly publication, and *Yachting and Boating Monthly*. An accomplished artist, he regularly exhibited at the Walker Gallery in Liverpool, and many times at the Royal Academy. He was well known and respected locally, with a reputation as a raconteur and wit. Very recently new pontoons in Scarborough Harbour were named after him, a fitting tribute to a man of many talents, but most especially remembered for his little canoe yawls. He suffered from failing health in his later years and finally died of heart failure in July 1917, and his death was much lamented by his friends and associates.

Strange designed his first boat, *Cherub*, in 1888 for his own use, she was a typical heavy cutter with a transom stern, and unusually she had two centreplates; he sailed her for several seasons, commenting favourably on the centreplate arrangement, but he did not repeat the experiment. His first commissioned design was probably the *Wren*, of 1889, a small cruiser with a gaff yawl rig and a small cabin. The cabin had a lifting roof and she was a little over fifteen feet long, again with a transom stern. Design details and a brief account of her sailing abilities were published in December of that year in the weekly *The Field*.

Other boats were to follow, one of the most well known was the 1909 design *Betty,* an auxiliary cutter of 48 feet overall, subsequently renamed *Tally Ho,* and in the ownership of Lord Stalbridge she was to win the 1927 Fastnet race in atrocious weather conditions when all others, including the famous Le Havre pilot cutter *Jolie Brise,* had retired save *La Goleta*, an American 70-foot schooner. In the days before specialist design of offshore racing yachts this was a considerable achievement.

With racing boats a number of different factors contribute to boat speed: primarily stability, weight and wetted surface area, but a fine entry and a fine run aft had became accepted as one of the pre-requisite for good performance. This increased knowledge of hydrodynamics led to faster and (mostly) better boats, but it was not without relevance to the design of a cruiser. An easily driven hull is desirable and a

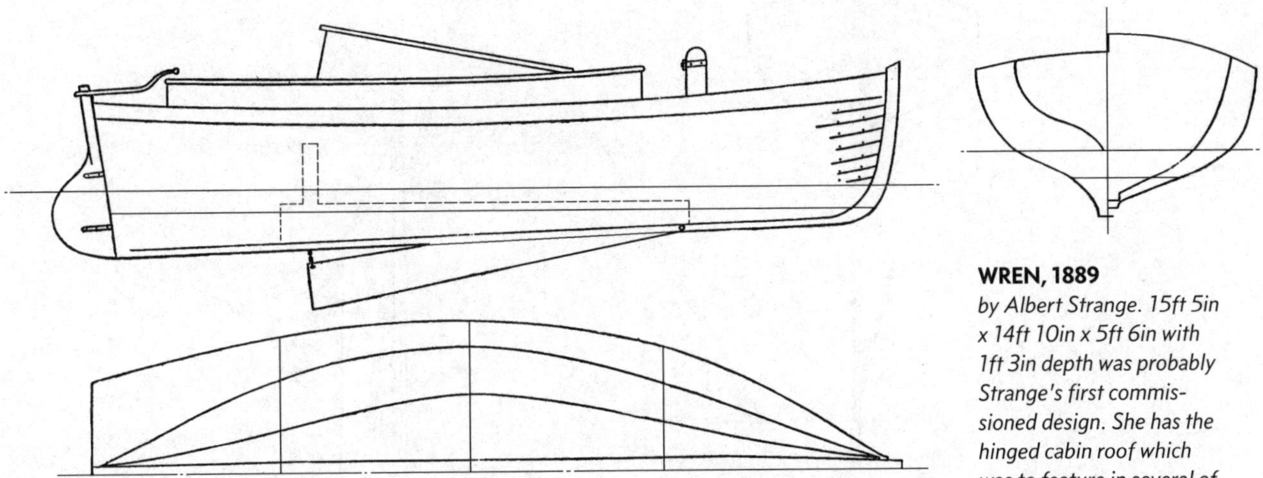

WREN, 1889

by Albert Strange. 15ft 5in x 14ft 10in x 5ft 6in with 1ft 3in depth was probably Strange's first commissioned design. She has the hinged cabin roof which was to feature in several of his designs, along with the long shallow centre plate under the cabin floor with a tube extension to take the lifting tackle well above the waterline.

canoe hull is exactly that. Thus original design thinking, previously confined to the racing yachts of the rich and famous, began to percolate down to more humble and affordable craft.

Ethel of 1888, one of four boats of that name designed by George Holmes, was built by J. A. Akester at Hornsea Mere, and marked a further departure from accepted wisdom in light canoe design. She was 13ft. overall with a much wider beam of 4ft. 6in. and out-performed her narrower cousins, including *Cassie* described earlier, by a considerable margin in local club racing. With her much increased volume she proved a more spacious and suitable type for cruising as well as racing. She was an inspirational design, marking a fundamental change in the hull form of the small canoe yawl, spawning several similar boats at the time and a number of modern replicas and derivatives.

The following year Holmes designed *Daisy,* a smaller version of a heavy Humber canoe yawl with an iron ballast keel and galvanised iron centre plate; she was designed for cruising with a two man crew and was another of the many Holmes boats built by Akester. *Daisy*'s antecedents are working boats and the likes of *Vital Spark* and *Viking* rather than the much lighter canoes and kayaks. She was based on Hornsea Mere

VITAL SPARK, c1880

by Sam Bond, Birkenhead. A little larger than the original Mersey Canoe Yawls, which started around 1877, at 18ft x 17ft 9in x 5ft with a draught of 2ft 2in, displacement of 1 ton 13 cwt., carrying a sail area of 178 sq. ft. but for racing it would have been about 300 sq. ft. She was rigged with a small jib, and was a clear development from working craft, rather than true canoes. She had 4½ cwt. of lead on the keel and carried a further 4½ cwt. internally. Later versions were larger, around 20ft, with another 1 cwt. of ballast added along with centre plates, no doubt to improve windward performance.

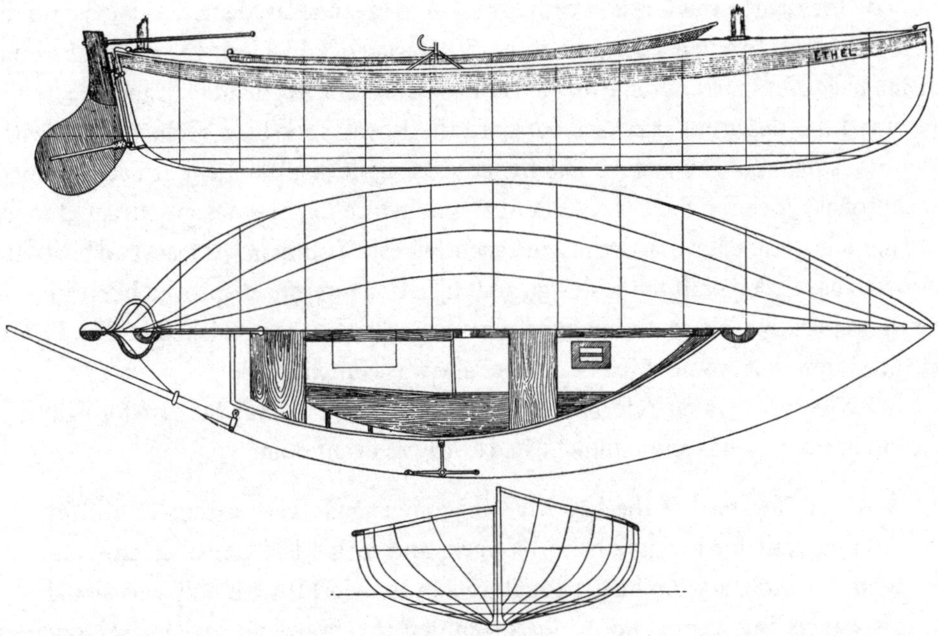

ETHEL, 1888
by George Holmes. At 13ft x 4ft 6in, the maximum length which would fit inside a railway car at the time. I can vouch for her sailing qualities as she was the basis for my design Sara.

and also undertook continental cruising, including Holland and Belgium in 1893 and Denmark in 1894.

Of all the luminaries in the evolution of the canoe yawl Albert Strange, for his practical, enlightened and imaginative approach, stands head and shoulders above the rest; he is generally regarded as the father of the type, even though he came to it rather late, in 1891. In addition to George Holmes, significant contributors included Sam Bond on the Mersey, Turk of Kingston-upon-Thames, and G. Umfreville Laws and J. Pain Clark, both of London.

By now we have seaworthy canoe yawls derived from heavier working boat types, and sailing canoes getting beamier and heavier. Canoes with fixed keels had appeared, and the centre plate became established. These two types began to merge and evolve, thanks in part to communications conducted via the contemporary yachting press.

The first canoe yawl design with his soon to become 'trademark' canoe counter stern was Albert Strange's design No. 4, of 1891, one of which was the little *Ethel* built in 1894 by R. Kemp of Oulton Broad, near Lowestoft, for Reginald H. Calvert. Strange presented the design as part of a paper to the Royal Yorkshire Yacht Club in early 1892; the subject of the lecture was the case for light displacement cruisers, a fairly revolutionary idea for the time. Like *Mosquito* before her the design attracted more than her fair share of criticism from the yachting establishment. At least two boats are known to have been built to the design and, like *Mosquito*, she disproved her critics. A lengthy report by Calvert on her suitability as a cruiser was published in *The Yachtsman* in March 1897, some three years after she was launched.

In his lecture Strange referred to R. T. McMullen in making his case for light displacement canoe yawls and I think he had a very relevant point:

> "I am aware that the late Mr McMullen made very extensive cruises in large craft for a single hand to work, and in his last cruise of all managed to handle a 5-ton lugger (of all rigs in the world) with only occasional assistance. But it must not be forgotten that this brave old sea-king seldom or never entered a harbour, spending night after night at sea, and that he was moreover a man of marvellous physical power and endurance. Yet even he, as his diary shows, was really much overworked, and I have little doubt that the exertion of working alone so large a craft hastened his lonely end.

Ethel was a significant departure from accepted wisdom, and heralded the beginning of the light displacement canoe yawl specifically designed for cruising. Strange explained the logic behind his thinking as follows (his italics):

> "The really important point is to get as large a craft as can be moved *under oars* in a calm and in harbours by a *single hand*. Not moved at great speed, but the boat must be light enough to be *rowed*, and this consideration fixes the type and the displacement to a very great extent. That a fairly

VIKING, 1886

by John Hamilton Jr. 18ft x 17ft 7in x 5ft x 2ft 5in, similar dimensions to Vital Spark, but of higher displacement at 1 ton 13 cwt. They differed in underwater form, she was a little deeper with an iron centre plate and another 1¾ cwt of ballast, plus another 1½ cwt for the plate. She carried 160 sq. ft. of sail, again with a small jib, but for racing a large balanced lug of 180 sq. ft.. Built of larch on American elm with battened seams, and oak floors. She was considered a better sea-boat altogether.

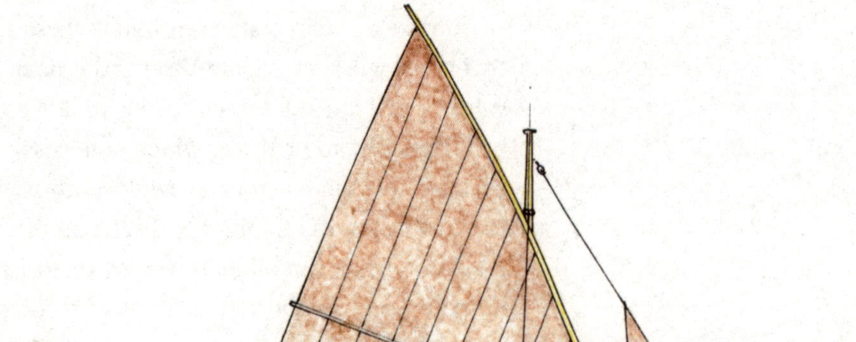

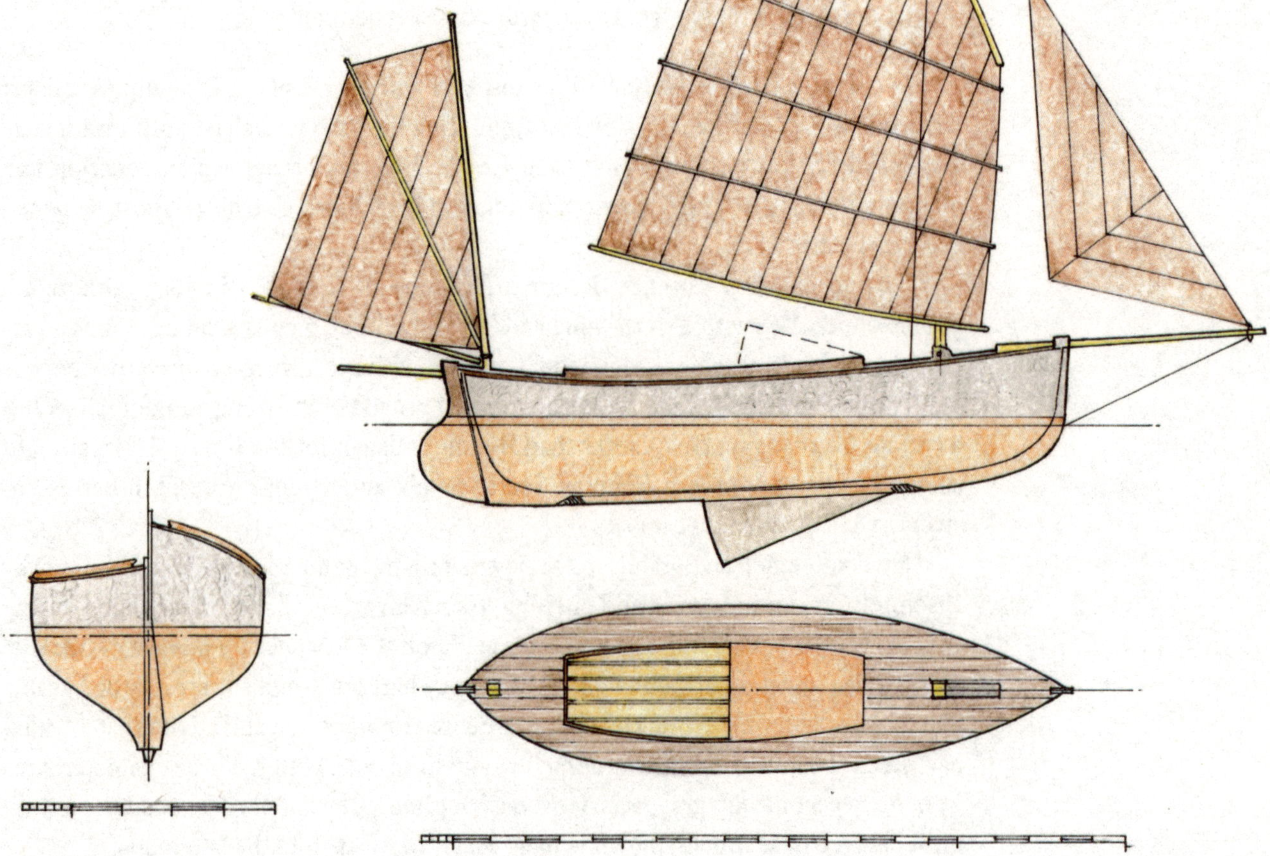

> seaworthy and fast craft even under these conditions is proved by the fact that the smaller fishing craft from Aberdeen to Harwich do not, as a general rule, exceed a displacement of 1½ tons, though they are generally manned by a crew of two or three, which is necessitated by the type of fishing they practise. Yet the Aberdeen yawls and those at Dunbar, the winter cobles of the east coast, the Cromer and Sherringham boats and the Southwold and Aldboro' punts can all be rowed by one man for short distances and about harbours, and yet these small craft go through as much bad weather at times as the stoutest single-hand sailor will care to encounter.

Ethel combines a canoe body with a fixed keel and centre plate; she unquestionably descends from Nautilus No. 5 and Rothion. She has heavier ballast both on the keel and inside. She is also very well thought out in terms of rig, accommodation and equipment which Strange describes in detail in his lecture. A truly purpose designed cruising boat.

The second boat Strange designed for himself, *Cherub II* in 1893, although a double ender (i.e., with a stern-hung rudder) rather than having a canoe counter, carried the light displacement idea which started with No. 4 further forward; she was built with a light double-skin construction and proved both strong and durable. With a curved overhanging bow, rather than the more usual, for the time at least, straight stem, she was built by Jas. Frank in Scarborough, and Strange cruised in her extensively over a number of years.

He commented favourably on the bow overhang 'of inestimable value in a seaway absolutely preventing diving and pitching to such an extent that on no occasion during the windy six weeks did any heavy water come on the foredeck'. The rake of her keel was also his salvation in an incident in Blakeney harbour when she struck the bar in a bit of a blow when entering. He also commented on her stern and added that a 'Jullanar' stern (a canoe counter as on *Ethel*) would have been better. These characteristics went on to become integral parts of his design philosophy and he described her as 'my most beloved boat'. She is known to have survived a least into the late 1940s.

ETHEL, 1891

by Albert Strange. 20ft 7in x 18ft x 6ft 6in with a depth of 2ft, carrying 169 sq ft of sail.
She is a little beamier than some of his later designs, and had a hollow bow which he described as 'weak' and did not replicate.

In 1895 he designed *Wa-Wa*, a heavy Humber yawl for Henry Hayes, another HYC member. A little larger than *Daisy,* she was a very capable sea boat built, like *Cherub II*, by Frank at Scarborough. Hayes took her to Holland in 1896. In 1897 she was sold to a Leslie Clift and Hayes and a paid hand undertook a sale/delivery cruise to her new home in Burnham-on-Crouch. The voyage started on 19 April and it took until 18 May to complete, bad weather bedevilling their efforts and causing her to be harbour-bound for several days on two occasions in a very uncomfortable and arduous trip. She was sold on to a new owner in Plymouth in 1902 and was last heard of in Weymouth in 1913.

By now the canoe yawl had developed into various sub-types; there were two quite distinct categories, which I have called 'heavy' and 'light' for convenience. Thus, the likes of *Vital Spark* and *Viking* are of heavy displacement for their length, and of working boat origin, whereas No. 4 and *Cherub II* are of relatively light displacement for their length and are descended from the canoe. The other distinction which needs to be drawn is in the hull shape. Of the previously mentioned quartet, I consider that three of them are more correctly described as double-enders, derived from working boats and only one, No. 4, is a true canoe hull, directly descended from the early North American canoes; but others may disagree.

Another cladistic difficulty that occurs when describing a canoe yawl is that many of them are, to the design purist, ketches; i.e., their rudder post sits behind the mizzen mast, not before it. However, although the term 'ketch' may be well-defined, 'yawl' is less so, and it is the relative areas of mizzen sail to main which justifies the appelation 'yawl'.

The little canoe yawls saw extensive cruising both at home and abroad, particularly across to Holland, to where regular steamer services sailed from Hull. Humber Yawl Club members started cruising in company on the Dutch inland waters around the late 1880s, adventurous for the time, shipping their little boats over on the steamers, spending several weeks cruising and camping in most summers. By the mid 1890s they numbered in double figures and included not only canoe yawls but the delightful so called 'houseboats'; the voluminous cabins on these charming little vessels provided a level of luxury not enjoyed by the canoe yawl 'campers'.

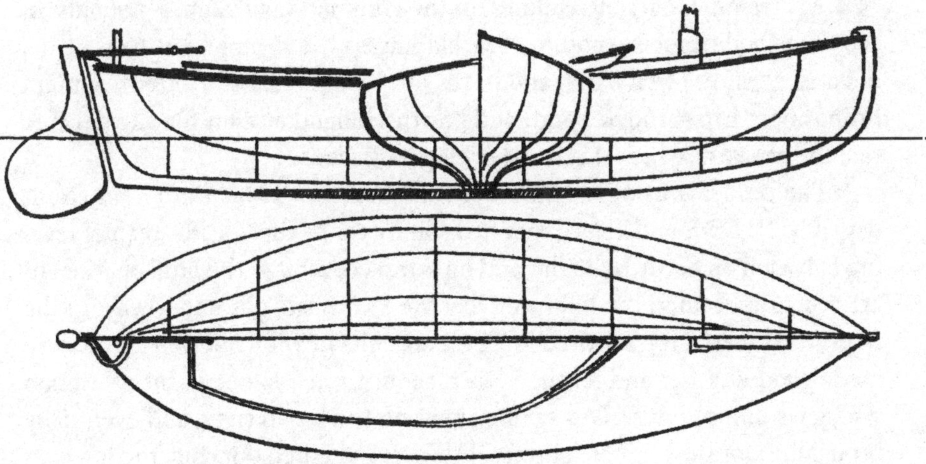

DAISY, 1889
by George Holmes. 18ft x 16ft 10in x 5ft 3in drawing 1ft 4in; a smaller version of the heavy Humber yawls. She would have carried about 200 sq ft of sail.

Many of the foregoing illustrations depict vessels with a fully battened lug mainsail, and often the mizzen as well. At the Humber Yawl Club this was known as 'Club Rig' and was very popular at the time. Close-hauled, a lugsail has a similar performance to a gaff, but when running and reaching it is a much more powerful sail, a fact which did not go unnoticed by 18th and 19th century smugglers when they changed to the type. The use of battens, generally in bamboo, made the task of reefing much quicker and easier and also gave the sails a better shape when reefed, important factors especially when racing these little craft with such large sail areas. Modern materials such as carbon fibre make the rig worthy of a second look and one has only to look at Nigel Irens' *Roxanne* design to appreciate that it can also be a very elegant rig indeed.

The following is an edited account of one of these Humber Yawl Club summer cruises which took place over 10 days in 1889; it was published in *The Model Yachtsman & Canoeist* in April 1891. It was written by H Wilmer, a R.C.C. member, and the 'the Editor' referred to was George Holmes, responsible for the canoeing section of the magazine. The boats include *Doris* 17ft x 4ft. 3in., built by Turk of Kingston-upon-Thames, a 'Cassy' type *Sea Gull,* along with *Viking* and *Ethel*.

"My friend, George F. Holmes, of the Humber Yawl Club, is not only an accomplished canoeist (nothing like kidding to the Editor), but he is also a devoted admirer of Holland, and it was in consequence of a letter from him proposing a trip through South and North Holland and on the Zuyder Zee that the cruise of which this is a short log took place.

The rendezvous of the little fleet of canoe yawls was Rotterdam. Sunday, July 21. *Doris* and her skipper had come over by the G.E.R. steamer leaving Harwich on Saturday night, and on Sunday evening, the Hull contingent arrived. About noon the following day the four boats got under way up the river Maas bound for Dordrecht. There was lots of wind but well abeam. We made good weather and reached Dort. about three o'clock in the afternoon where we amused ourselves sailing about on the broad river, and eventually brought up for the night in a pretty little creek situated opposite the town on the other side of the river.

The following day, July 23, we left Dort. about 11 a.m. and returned down the Maas as far as its junction with the Ijssel. The wind was SW and as our course after passing the mouth of the Lek was westerly we had a long beat for some four or five miles till we reached the mouth of the Ijssel so that once in the river we glided along past pleasant little homesteads where the children rushed out to see us pass, overhauling ponderous Schuyts with their quaint, old-world sails and bluff bows. On nearing Gouda we were overtaken by a sharp thunderstorm ushered in by a violent wind squall, some of my friends got very wet, as the oilies were snugly stowed away forward, and one of the fleet nearly turned turtle during the squall.

We reached the lock gates at Gouda, communicating with the Canals, in a perfect deluge of rain. The rain ceased as suddenly as it started and we were admitted into the big lock in company with several Schuyts, and here the skipper of the *Doris* was commissioned to go ashore and go through all the necessary formalities for admission into the canals. After making our way through intricate channels we eventually found a resting place for the night outside the town, and within a narrow creek heading up to a mill. Soon the tents were up and the merry kettle gaily singing, but a sad thing occurred.

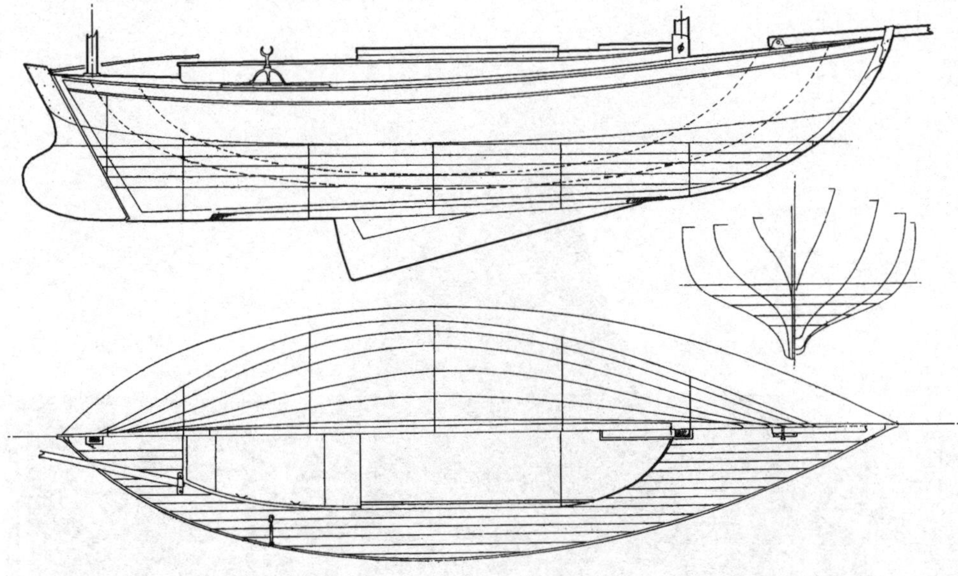

CHERUB II, 1893
by Albert Strange.
20ft 2in x 17ft 7in x 5ft 10in x 1ft 9in, she displaced 1.9 tons and carried 249 sq ft of sail. Very much an extension of the thinking behind Ethel of 1891. A double-ender, ie with stern-hung rudder; Strange later observed that a canoe counter would have been 'much better', nevertheless she was his favourite boat.

Our friend, the Editor, who has a delicate digestion, was found to be entirely 'off his feed'. Even *Doris*'s refined and high class cooking would not induce him to make a good dinner. I may say that the Editor's digestion was a source of much anxiety to me during the remainder of the cruise, and led to my adopting for his benefit a higher standard of cooking.

The following morning we made a late start, as the attraction of Gouda with its magnificent church and quaint streets kept us busy. However, noon saw us again under way, and as the wind had gone round NW we had a peg to windward up the narrow canal known as Gouwe. Our intention was to work up the Gouwe as far as its junction with the old Rhine at Alphen, and then to follow that river to Leyden. Turning to windward up a narrow channel is however slow and tedious work, and it was quite four p.m. before we found ourselves on the old Rhine. The scenery along the banks of the river is very picturesque, on either side are private houses with gardens leading down to the water's edge,

CHERUB II
in Scarborough harbour

alongside of which are moored private Schuyt yachts resplendent with polished iron and brass work.

It was now getting late, and finding that Leyden was still some five miles to windward we decided, after a careful inspection of the map, to take a lateral canal leading up to a lake called Brassem Meer, and abandon our intention of putting in at Leyden. Once through the little lock we bore away to the eastward and made a quick passage with wind on the quarter as far as Brassem Meer, and skirting the west side of the lake brought up for the night at a little village called Koelof Arendsveen.

The little village at which we camped is quite out of the run of the ordinary tourist, and amused us amazingly. The principal and only occupation of its inhabitants appears to be the cultivation of gherkins and kidney beans. The main street of the village is bounded on one side by a narrow canal, on the opposite side of which are the private residences of the inhabitants. Each house, which stands in its own garden, is veritably its owner's castle as it is approached by a swing bridge pivoted on the garden side. Anyone desiring to cross over picks up a boat hook which is chained to the ground on the street side opposite each house, and with this he pulls the swing bridge over. When I say that the canal is about ten feet wide only, it will be seen that this is not a big operation.

The following morning it was blowing very fresh and there was quite a sea running on Brassem Meer, and we crossed it with reefed canvas to the NE corner and found ourselves in the canal which skirts the whole of the western side of the once famous Haarlem Meer. Some of the pumping stations by which it is now kept in the condition of dry land are situated along the canal and form very imposing structures. We reached Haarlem about four p.m. and as the canal runs through the town, and there are a number of bridges, we found it advisable to lower our masts and scull the boats through.

After passing through the town we brought up for the night in a little dyke on the left hand side just below the Railway Bridge. It is not safe to bring up for the night in the canal itself as there is a good deal of navigation going on at all times. We moored in a dyke which led up to the Amsterdam gate, one of the old fortified city gates so familiar in continental towns. We had hardly commenced setting our tent when a heavy thunderstorm broke. It had been brewing for some time and when once started lasted about two hours. Fortunately it assisted in flushing the dyke in which we were lying.

We spent the following morning in Haarlem, the Editor sketching the water gate, and break-fasting afterwards with *Doris* in a typical Dutch tavern where we were regaled on eggs and coffee, and cheese sandwiches, and roaming about the town which is full of interesting sights. We left Haarlem

CHERUB II
in the Looe Overfalls
off Selsey Bill, Sussex,
by Albert Strange

about two o'clock in the afternoon for Zaandam. We worked up the canal as far as Spaarndam, where we were admitted through a lock into the North Sea Canal. Our course was now to the eastward in the direction of Amsterdam, and then northward up the river Zaan.

We reached Zaandam about five p.m., and sailed about on the fine stretch of river drying our sails, which had hardly recovered the wetting of the previous night. We moored for the night at a ship builder's yard on the south side of the river, and after making everything snug we went into Amsterdam by the seven o'clock steamer and there enjoyed ourselves. We did not take long to find the Hotel Krasnopolski and enjoy a square meal, such

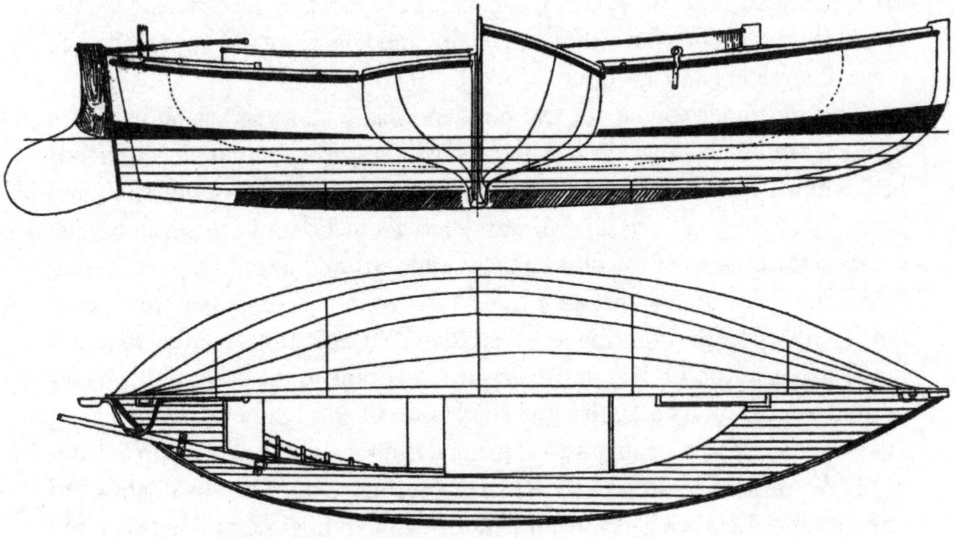

WA-WA, c1895
by Albert Strange.
19ft 3in x 18ft 8in x 5ft 11in x 1ft 7in;
she had a 6 cwt iron keel and carried 220 sq ft of sail.
A heavy Humber Canoe Yawl, built by Jas. Frank of Scarborough.

as the Editor's delicate organisation even could not object to. We returned to Zaandam by the last train.

The following morning the wind was blowing hard from NW, and we had a very wet and disagreeable turn to windward up the Zaan. The houses on each side of the river obstructed the wind very much so that sailing was anything but pleasant, the wind coming now and again in fierce squalls and veering round three or four points. We were bound for Purmerend, and after about eight miles this sort of cuss work our course bore away NE, and then on to the North Holland Canal due E, so that the latter part of our journey was made with a fair wind and in smooth water. It blew very hard however all day, and we found it best to sail under single reef.

We reached Purmerend about five o'clock, and after lowering masts and sculling through the town we brought up for the night in a side canal and rigged our tent. Distance run 23 kilometres. The following day being Sunday we decided to rest. We were moored for the night alongside a path which appeared to be a sort of promenade for the youths and children of the place.

We were much annoyed by them, and obliged to move to the other side of the creek; this was about the only place in Holland where we did not receive the greatest kindness and attention

We got under way about five p.m. and had a short sail as far as Edam where we moored alongside a paddock in which a Mill is situated. My friends had camped here before, and the Miller at once gave his permission, and treated us with great civility. We wandered about Edam in the evening, listened to the chimes of the church bells, and returned to our ships by moonlight. The following day we were to part from the *Viking* as they were going north, and we were returning to Amsterdam. We spent the evening together in the saloon of the *Viking*, smoked cigars and drank to the crew of the *Viking* in tumblers of Curaçao: such is the abundance of good things in Holland.

The following morning we left in good time as we had a long trip in front of us. We were now close to the Zuyder Zee, and a short sail in a light wind brought us to the lock gates. After passing through the lock and between the timber break-waters we found ourselves on the Zuyder Zee. Not a breath of air was moving, not a ripple to be seen on its glassy surface. Dotted at intervals over its broad expanse were Schuyts hailing from the many little fishing ports on the shores. The scene was enchanting but we had no wind and without this we should have no chance of getting through our day's programme.

We decided to bathe and as we were dressing a light wind sprang up and we made our way into Vollendam. We wandered about this quaint old fishing town and then sailed out of the little harbour bound across to the island of Marken. There was a nice little breeze and a pleasant ripple as we ran with wind dead aft across to Marken. Half-an-hour was spent at this quaint and picturesque spot, and we sailed across with a reaching wind to Monnickendam, and arrived at Broek-in-Waterland about six p.m. Distance run this day about 20 kilometres.

On reaching Broek we moored for the night alongside a little grass paddock, on which some hayricks were standing. We were soon surrounded by an eager crowd of men and women. Their delight and amusement at everything they saw was unbounded, and re-called some of the incidents de-

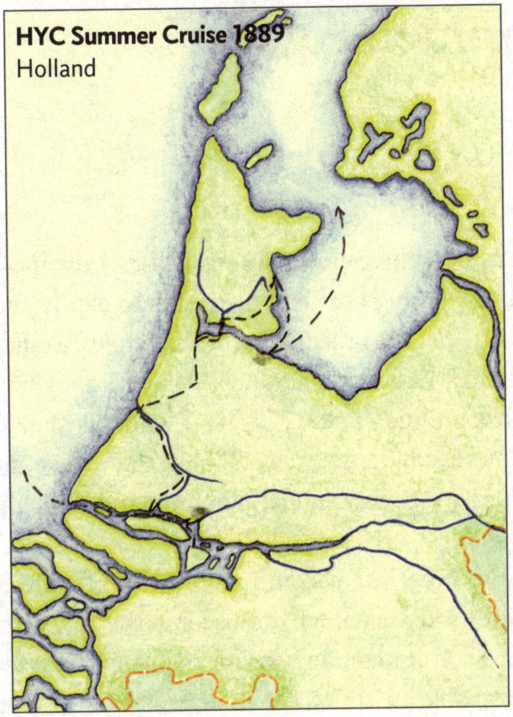

scribed by Mr MacGregor in his canoe cruises. They tasted our coffee, tried our English biscuits and enjoyed everything we submitted to them with the exception of some oatmeal cakes belonging to the Editor. We received a visit from the Burgomaster, Mr. Rhems, and he undertook to call us early on the following morning so that we might be shown everything of interest.

The next morning, our last day in Holland, we accompanied Mr. Rhems and his son round the village, saw the model cheese farm, the national schools, church, and everything of interest, and after receiving an introduction to the rest of Mr. Rhems's family we sailed into Amsterdam and left the same evening by the S.S. *European* for Hull. This trip lasted altogether about 10 days, and from first to last was the most enjoyable one of its kind which the writer has experienced.

4 The Golden Age

We have now seen how the canoe yawl evolved as a distinct type from its early canoe, kayak and working boat origins; it was to evolve further to fill the role of fully-fledged and very elegant cruising yacht. Examples would be produced from the boards of a number of designers, although Albert Strange and George Holmes were probably the most prolific. These 'Canoe Yachts' as they came to be known, were mostly small, around about 25 feet overall, but there were much larger versions designed and built. They were all of similar hull form and came in centreboard, fixed and fin bulb keel versions.

By now auxiliary motors had become more available and, more importantly, reliable, and installations were eventually to become the rule rather than the exception. Internal levels of creature comfort within the cabin increased greatly as more equipment became available in the wake of the increasing popularity of recreational sailing. New man-made materials were also beginning to make an appearance; linoleum was starting to replace the canvas which was generally used for deck coverings on the cheaper boats, where traditional laid teak planking was not an economic option.

One of the earliest examples of the canoe yawl in its final form with a canoe counter was *Otter* of 1898, designed by Albert Strange, who had built upon his much earlier but very similar design, the little *Ethel* of 1891 and turned it into a larger and much more sophisticated offering for use on Canada's St. Lawrence River. She was built for an R. J. Durley, a member of both the Royal St. Lawrence Yacht Club, and the Humber Yawl Club, in 1899 by A. Lake, in Longueil, PQ, just opposite the Port of Montreal.

At 7ft 6in she was considerably beamier than his usual designs, perhaps following a local preference. In his book *Albert Strange, Yacht Designer & Artist* John Leather

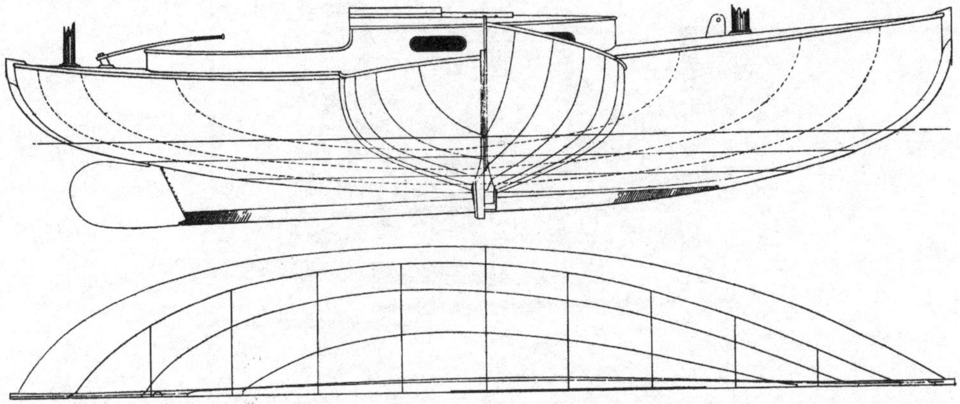

OTTER, 1889
by Albert Strange.
25ft x 22ft x 7ft 6in x 2ft 2in, with a little over 400 sq ft of sail.

commented on 'a more powerful craft… for a much greater river than the Humber' an incorrect assumption which led him to be critical with some aspects of the design.

The tidal effects of the St. Lawrence cease at Quebec City about 200 miles upstream of the river mouth. The limit of navigation is the Port of Montreal, another 150 miles upstream and situated below the Lachine rapids. Above these rapids is the shallow and tranquil Lake St. Louis, about 10 miles long and 4 miles wide; this is where the Royal St Lawrence Yacht Club is based, and this was *Otter*'s home water. This makes much more sense of the shoal water design which she clearly is. She was last heard of in Montreal, in 1921.

Interestingly a little later in January 1901 *The Yachtsman* contained an item headed *Small Yacht Motors* reprinted from the Ohio *Motor Vehicle Review*, describing the installation in her of an auxiliary engine during the spring of 1900, which was very early. It was accompanied by a drawing and a description of the motor which was described as a single cylinder 'Wolverine' gasoline engine, with a 4in bore and stroke; it was bench tested at 2.2bhp and consumed 2¼ pints per hour. Running at a fairly ideal propeller speed of 390–400rpm there was no need for a gearbox, and it appears to have been a very simple and easily maintained installation, from which we could learn today.

By now parallel developments in recreational sailing had spawned some rather unusual craft where accommodation, rather than sea-keeping ability or performance,

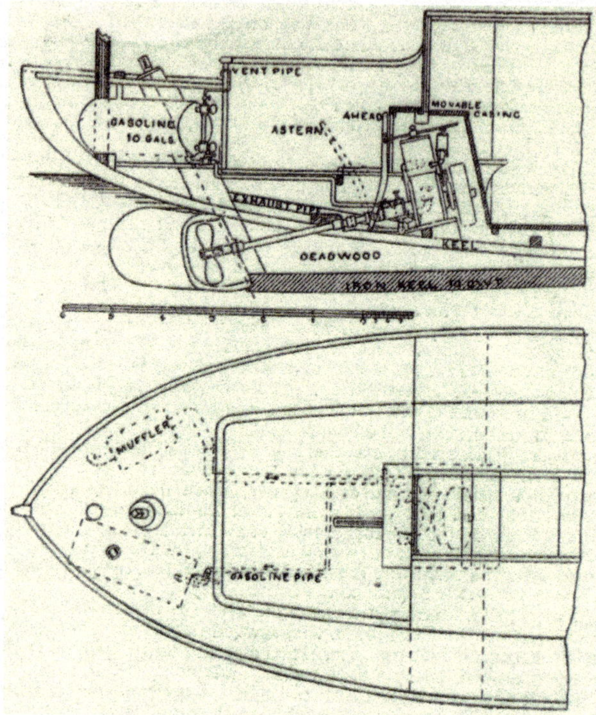

OTTER
Engine details, 1900

was the prime consideration. This particular criterion has repeated itself in modern designs to some extent and will be discussed in detail later. The first of these, the sailing houseboat, was a very odd-looking craft, basically a dinghy with a transom stern, with an over-large and rather ugly cabin. Utilitarian though it was, it provided a much greater level of personal comfort than was offered by a small canoe yawl with a tent. I must admit to having some sympathy with this point of view. These little craft also travelled abroad, and *Oompah* of 1895 accompanied a HYC cruise to Holland in 1896, and must have provided welcome shelter from time to time for the more Corinthian sailors.

In the latter part of 1900 in the correspondence columns of *The Yachtsman* there was a discussion on the subject of canoe yachts, which were by now an established type, following the publication of drawings of *Rani IV* designed by J Pain Clark. Sloop rigged with a large mainsail, and with a long overhanging boom, she was a beautiful design and Pain Clark's draughtsmanship is first rate. He described the design as follows:

> "Sir—Referring to the letter in your last issue from 'small cruiser' on the subject of canoe yachts, I enclose the lines of *Rani IV* which is being built for me by the Burnham Yacht Building Company, and may be of interest to single handers.
>
> I am afraid that I rather fail to see the point of the attack on canoe yachts made by the Canoeing editor of *The Field*. I have always considered that it was universally acknowledged, or, at any rate, by canoeists, that the best type of small boat for sea-going qualities was the canoe form of hull. There is no doubt that there is an increasing demand for small single-handed cruisers nowadays, and unless *The Field* wishes to discourage the sport entirely, and make out that no man is justified in leaving land-locked waters in a small boat, I do not see the force of its remarks.
>
> I was personally greatly influenced in designing *Rani IV* by observing the excellent sea-going qualities of the canoe yacht *Dimsie III*, designed by Mr G. U. Laws for Mr Norman S. Carr. Although only 20ft overall and 5ft 3in beam she is one of the best single-handers as regards sea-going qualities I have ever come across. She is wonderfully dry for her size, and in a strong breeze and moderate sea will compare favourably with much larger boats in point of speed and seaworthiness. She is certainly very pluckily handled by her owner, but even in the hands of the novice of whose welfare *The Field* is always so solicitous, I consider she would be safer than any boat of her size and displacement.
>
> The design of *Rani IV* has been prepared with a view to securing a stiff dry boat, and especially a good sea boat, with the maximum of accommodation and the minimum of displacement and sail area in order to ensure economy in building and maintenance, and simplicity and lightness of gear

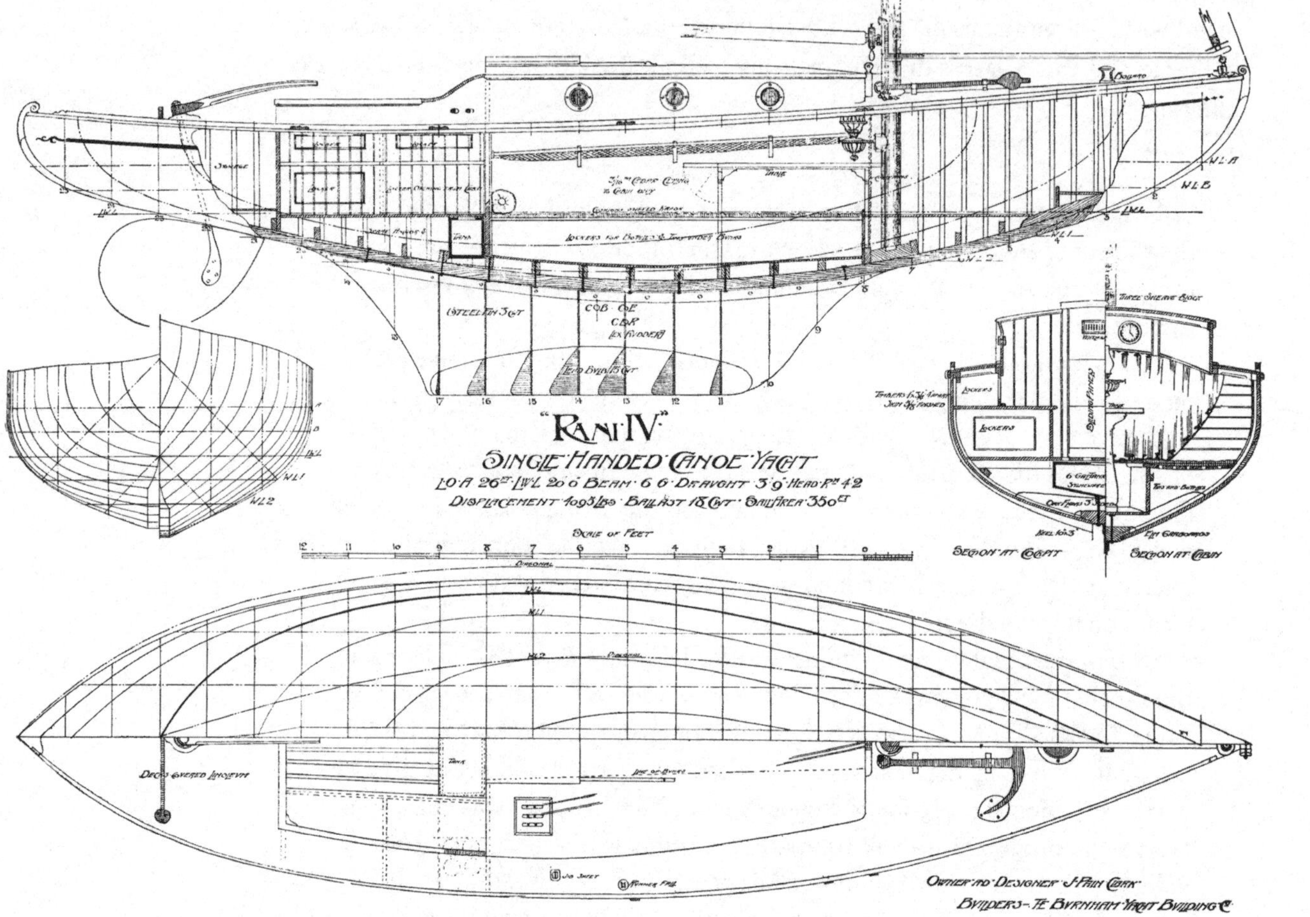

RANI IV, c1900

by J Pain Clark. 26ft x 20ft x 6ft 6in x 3ft 9in; she displaced a little over 1¾ tons and carried 350 sq ft of sail.

for ease in handling. Speed has been entirely subordinated to the above consideration, and the form of section with fin and bulb keel are adopted as the best means of obtaining the above combination. Some men would probably say, offhand and without consideration, that the boat is of those bulb-fin racing machine abortions. This, however, is mere prejudice, and the type has been adopted after practical experience in my former boat *Rani III*, as being more seaworthy, and having more accommodation for her cost and displacement, than a V section boat would have.

I have adopted the sharp stern because I consider that it is an improvement for a small cruiser, as it gives her a grip of the water aft and does away with a certain amount of wildness on the run caused by a long flat counter riding on a following sea. At the same time I have endeavoured to retain the advantages of the counter by keeping the overhang low and getting the benefit of the increased length of waterline when the hull is heeled. I am personally very much opposed to long overhangs, which I think are never worth their weight and windage, but some overhang is no doubt necessary in a good sea boat, and I have adopted the sharp stern as the best form I know of.

The design, I think, does not need much explanation, as the notes on same are full. I have decided on a movable pump with India-rubber tubes, one of which can be led into the lee bilge or amidships, as desired. This form of pump can be obtained with a stirrup for the foot, and, of ample power for a boat of *Rani*'s size, it does away with the difficulty of only being able to pump when on a level keel. The cushions will be stuffed with kapok, which is beautifully soft, and combines the advantages of horsehair as regards damp, with great buoyancy, thus making effective lifebuoys as well as cushions.

All the halyards will of course lead aft, and the anchor will always be kept stocked on deck ready for use, one end of the stock dropping into a galvanized iron tube passing through the deck. This was first brought out by Mr Laws (to whom I am indebted for several suggestions in connection with the design) and is of the greatest value in a single-hander. I have frequently found it awkward having to go forward and stock the anchor single-handed in a crowded anchorage. The bunks will be formed to a curve as shown on the drawings and will be laid with spaces between the battens to ventilate the underside of the cushions.

This was soon followed by a letter from Albert Strange along with a design #63, dated December 1900. Letter and design had lain unnoticed for over 100 years and were recently rediscovered to fill in a major gap in the evolution of the canoe yawl, coming right in between the early boats and the later more refined designs. The letter is not reproduced in full, but the first part gives a nice résumé of the type and its suitability for purpose:

> "Sir—I have pleasure in sending you herewith the plans of a canoe-yacht of the centre-board type which may possibly be found of interest to your readers. At least it is interesting to note that these little craft are likely to spread in America as much as they have in England, but the probability is that, in the hands of our cousins across the pond, they are likely to develop in beam to a much greater extent than is generally the case with us, and Mr. Lansing's latest idea is to have a 7ft 6in beam on the same lwl, and the same displacement, as my present design. This means, of course, much greater internal accommodation and initial stiffness; but I doubt very much whether such an amount of beam would pay in our waters, at any rate in coasting, my experience being that 6ft, or a few inches over, are the best proportions on a lwl of from 18 to 20ft, provided of course that the ballast is, in amount and position, sufficient to give the craft the necessary impetus and stability under canvas in disturbed water.
>
> A few remarks on the design may, perhaps, be of interest, especially as we have just had, from the board of Mr Pain Clark, so excellent an example of the canoe-yacht as a fin bulb keel craft. For general and exploring cruises in this part of the world, and also in Denmark and Holland (when the political atmosphere is clear enough to allow us to resume our cruises in the last-named), the centre-board boat of moderate draught has undoubted advantages. All along the coast on which (in England) the HYC men cruise

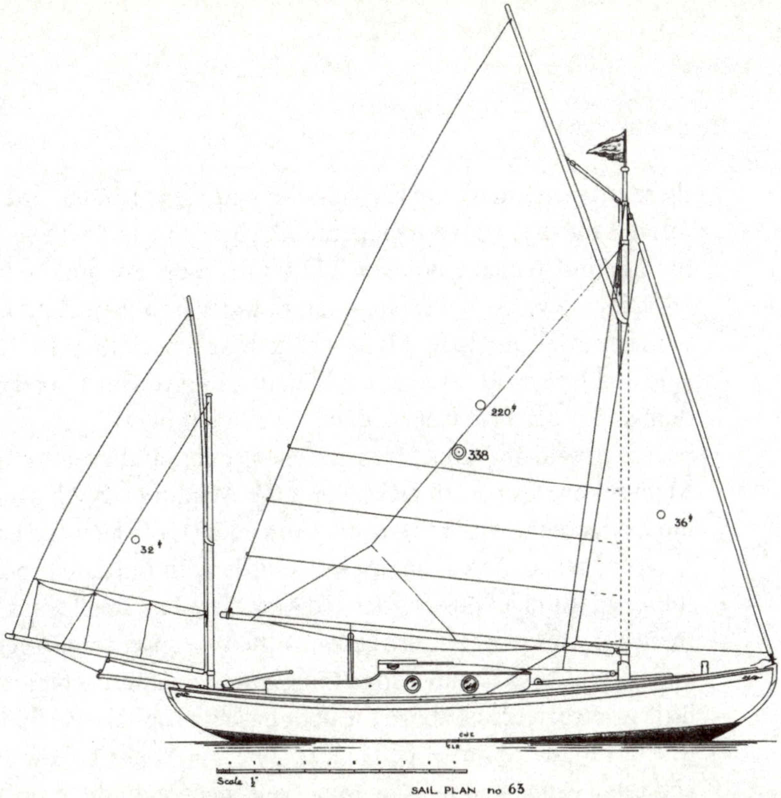

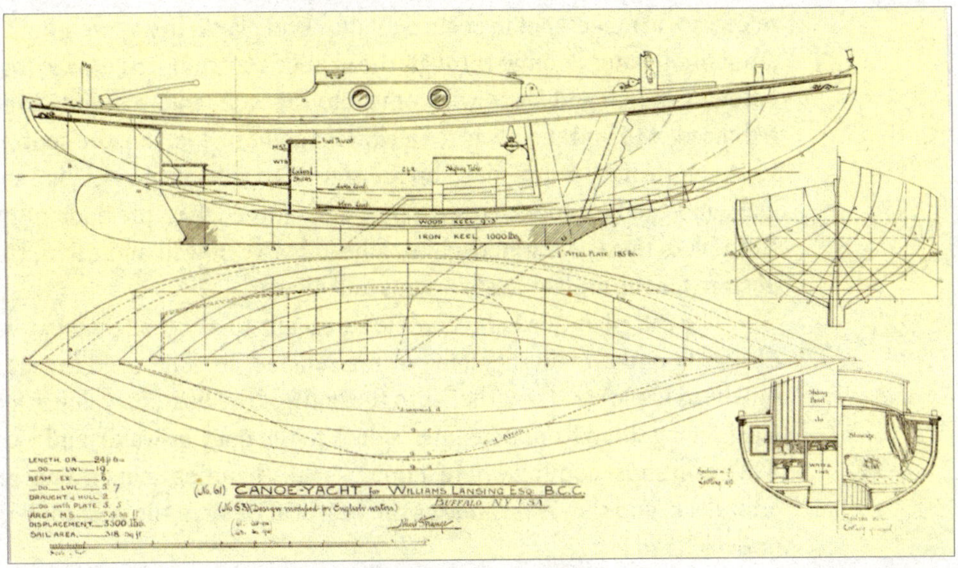

DESIGN No. 63, 1900

by Albert Strange. 24ft 6in x 19ft x 6ft x 2ft; she displaced 1.56 tons and carried 318 sq ft of sail. This design was subsequenty widened to 7ft 5in beam and became Leona. *The original sail plan was unclear; the one above was drawn by Iain Oughtred.*

there are many small dry harbours very good to visit, but often most uncomfortable for any boat with more than 2ft draught, and with very poor bottoms for legs. In Denmark and North Germany there are hundreds of small ports with, in many cases, only about 3ft of water into them, and in taking which, with any swell at all on, it is as well to have a bit if margin. And also in Holland and Friesland 2ft of fixed draught will give you a good deal more freedom and much less responsibility than anything deeper. Lastly the centre-board, all said and done, is an excellent pilot; and even in the Thames and Medway one can work tacks along the Maplin or Blyth sands a good deal more effectively with the c.b. pilot as a guide for 'touch and go.'

And when the c.b. interferes so little with the cabin room as it does in this case, the chief objection to it disappears. The small trunk through which the lever works comes just between the two spaces most generally used as berths, and thus ensures something remotely approaching to privacy. The little piece projecting above the floor makes a capital base for a shifting table. Practically the cabin space is clear. The watertight bulkhead between well and cabin is not a concession to nervous people on the score of safety, but a necessary arrangement in boats built on a keel plank. In any well-built raft the amount of water coming through the skin or centre-board case is (or should be) nil. But rain and spray will come into the well, and, without a watertight bulkhead, will find their way to the lowest point inside, i.e., the centre of cabin. A semi-rotary pump, fixed on the starboard side of the well, is enough for well, and can be connected with pipe and stop-cock to the body of the boat. But unless there is a watertight bulkhead between well and cabin, trouble is in store for the cruiser when it rains and blows.

The sail plan needs no comment, except to say that the boat will handle easily under mainsail alone, or mizzen and jib. The fixed thwart on this bulkhead is a great strengthener to the body of the boat, its value is felt when she is being lifted from a steamer's deck to the quay or water, and vice versa. The main sheet coming where it does is really handier than on a horse on the after deck, and the thwart makes the best seat of all in the boat for passenger or deck hand.

The compromise of 2ft draught and a plate works exceedingly well in practice, however much theory may be against it. I do not advocate it from a racing point of view, but to name but one instance of the weatherliness of a boat of this type, I remember, in the *Eel*, turning dead to windward from Høruphav to Bulk Point in the Baltic, about 33 nautical miles, in under two hours, double-reefed sail, and with a lee-going current. On the same cruise we turned down Flensborg Fjord, in company with a German revenue cruiser, schooner rigged, and held our own with him for some miles (we were under double reefed sail) until, in the wider parts of the fjord, the bigger sea and the longer reaches helped him to weather us. To borrow an expression I have somewhere seen applied to canoe yachts, the *Eel* is a somewhat 'clumped up' ship of 7ft beam and 19ft lwl, 2ft fixed draught, but her owner generally manages to get where he is bound to and when I have had the pleasure of sailing as deck hand on her, I have noticed that she has a habit of passing most cruising craft of her size and many bigger ones when it comes to a bout to windward.

This second letter sums up the thinking of the time in respect of these little canoe yawls rather nicely from a man by now considered an authority on the subject. The *Eel* referred to in the letter was designed by George Holmes for his own use; she was a small cruiser, and Holmes cruised extensively in her until 1912 when he sold her to his old friend Edward Hicks Oliver who was, like both Strange and Holmes, an artist of some ability.

These two designs were preceded by a couple of other canoe yachts; the first of these was *Snickersee* (1897) designed by the American W P Stephens. He lived in Bayonne, New Jersey at the time but was a member, albeit somewhat distant, of the Humber Yawl Club and corresponded regularly with both Albert Strange and George Holmes. He was a notable canoeist, designer and builder and wrote extensively on the subject and was later to be instrumental in saving a large part of Albert Strange's design drawing collection for posterity.

The design was published in the HYC Yearbook of 1898, Stephens writing:

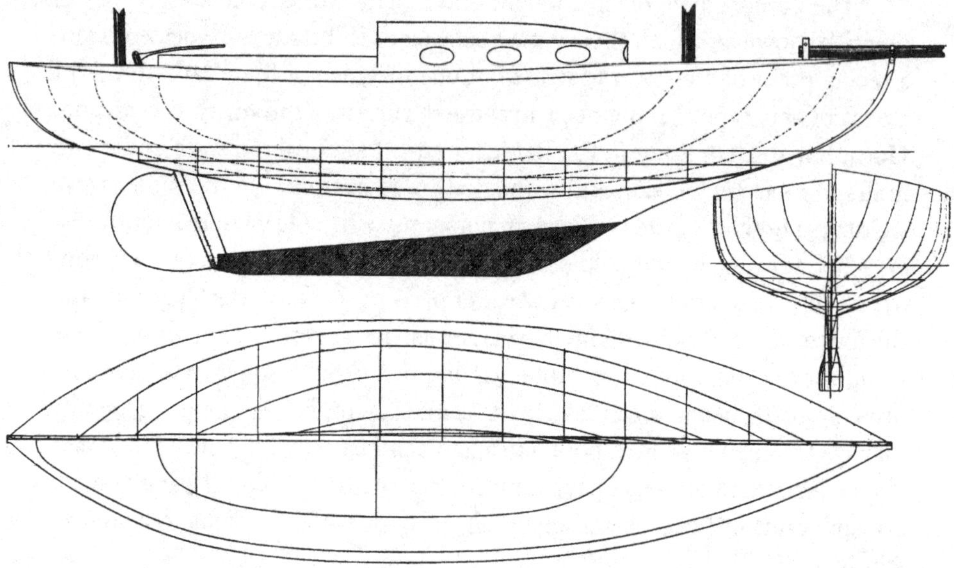

SNICKERSNEE, 1897
by W P Stephens

"To the Humber Yawl Club is due the credit for the development and perfection of a particular type of cruising canoe-yacht, which, by the familiar performances of *Eel*, *Cherub*, *Birdie*, and *Tavie II*, has given good reason for its existence. The merits of this type, with its moderate draft, internal space, and power derived from large displacement, are incontestable in theory and fully proven in practice by the many cruises of these boats and others. At the same time it must not be forgotten that the original canoe-yacht was distinctively a keel craft; and whatever objection may be urged by the adherents of the centre board type, the keel can still point to the cruises of the original yawl *Rob Roy*, of *Vital Spark*, the early Mersey canoe-yawls, and *Water Rat* and *Viper*.

This design is a study in the direction of the later development of the old Mersey type, being based, in fact, on a poor copy of *Vital Spark*, owned by the writer some years ago. In it an attempt has been made to utilize the modern ideas of form in producing a faster and far abler boat on about the same dimensions as the old *Vital Spark*; and for the same purpose of single-hand cruising. On a waterline 18 feet, which may be taken as the favourite size for this sort of craft, by virtue of the moderate overhangs and very full level lines, it has been possible to obtain a hull which will compare favourably in size with the yawl *Rob Roy* and the canoe-yacht *Viper* on much smaller nominal dimensions. At the same time the form is such as to give promise of an all-around advantage over the older boats in speed, handiness, and ease and power in a seaway.

If these results are not obtained, it must he laid to the individual defects of this particular design, and not to the type which it represents.

In working out the design, last fall, it scented that a double advantage could he gained by the short after overhang (which, though unusual, is not inconsistent with the canoe type) both in a better ending of the fore and aft lines, and in a secure step for the mizenmast well clear of the rudder head and tiller. It was believed at the time that this idea was original; and it is only lately that I have heard from "Cherub" of a similar plan first devised by him some years ago, but never put into practice.

This design is intended to be well within the ability of any single hander and at the same time to give reasonably good accommodation for two persons in a permanent cabin that shall be at all times dry and cosy. The draft of three feet, quite enough for power and lateral plane, is not too much for convenient use in many localities, and has certain advantages of its own as compared with the two feet of the centre board type. For one very important point, the middle of the cabin is left entirely clear, greatly increasing the room.

The construction is essentially that of a canoe, with flat bent keel, the fin being added after the hull is completed. The iron keel is of course bolted up through the deadwood of the fin and the main keel and floors. The head-room is 3ft 8ins, under roof of house, which is shown as 6ft long, leaving a cockpit 4ft 5ins long. The cockpit floor is shown below the L.W.L., but 4ins above the cabin floor. The bulkhead between cabin and cockpit is watertight throughout, and the sill of door may be carried up well above the L.W.L., or, if kept low for convenient passage in ordinary weather, a movable piece may

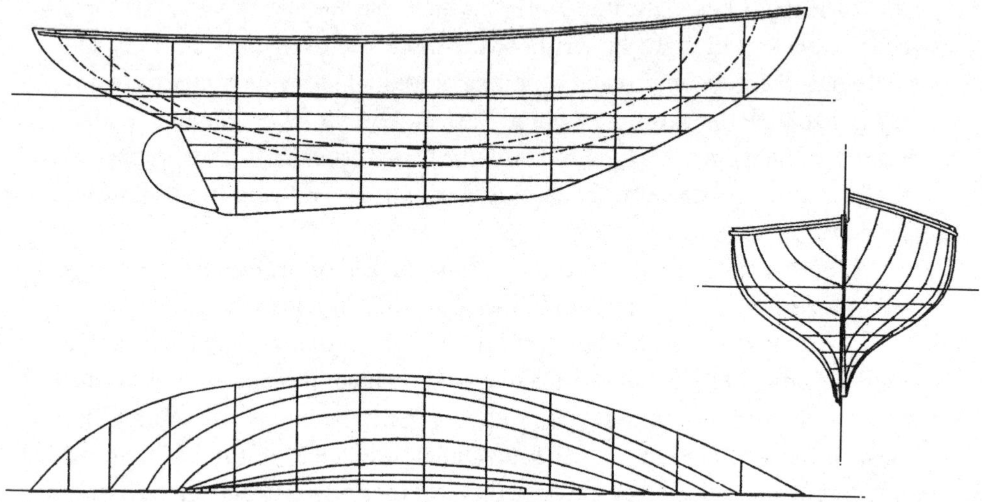

CATRIONA, 1898
by Louis Sanderson

he fitted below the doors proper, so nearly watertight as to prevent any rush of water to the cabin in the very remote contingency of the cockpit being flooded.

The sail plan of *Eel* seems to be very nearly perfect for cruising, both in general arrangement and details, and probably nothing better could be devised for this design in English waters. About Long Island Sound and New York Bay, in summer, a total area of 300 sq ft would be none too much with adequate arrangements for shortening sail quickly, and the tabernacle might well be dispensed with. The masts are shown as placed for such a rig. In English waters this might be reduced to less than 250 sq ft.

Stephens was later to regret the level keel on *Snickersee* after running aground and thereafter advocated the raked version favoured by Strange, who initially learnt of its value crossing Blakeney Bar in *Cherub II*.

Catriona (1898) was designed by Louis Sanderson, who was taught the rudiments of yacht design by Strange, and she was entered in *The Yachtsman* Design Competition of that year, being awarded 2nd prize. At the time some readers assumed incorrectly that *Catriona* was the first example of a canoe counter stern. In spite of having corresponded with Strange for some time Stephens was unaware of the design *Ethel* of 1891 so he developed the canoe counter stern in isolation, probably taking his inspiration (as presumably did Strange, having mentioned it when discussing *Cherub II* in correspondence related earlier) from *Jullanar* (1875), a 100-foot yawl built by John Harvey at Wivenhoe on the Essex coast. I also understand that a Sydney cutter 'Australia' (1858) had a similar stern but I cannot confirm if this was the case. In any event it was unquestionably Strange who developed it for the small cruising yacht.

The following is an extract from a cruise on the West coast of Scotland in 1909 undertaken by Robert Groves, a Humber Yawl Club member in Albert Strange design #70 *Sheila* (1903)—more of her later. Groves, also an artist, cruised these waters annually, and his sketches are particularly pleasing.

> "The cruise of 1909 was not nearly so sporting in character as that of the previous season when Stornoway was reached and many other romantic and far-distant spots were visited, more than half of the time being spent in the waters of Loch Fyne. The weather on the whole was good, very good as compared with what was experienced in England; and though the time spent north of Crinan was only eighteen days, several fresh and highly interesting anchorages were added to Sheila's list.
>
> Leaving Tarbert, Loch Fyne on July 17th, our first run down to Skipness and back to Buck Bay, was in the nature of a trial trip on which any weak spot in the gear would be revealed. The next day was spent in Buck Bay, which we left in the evening for Tarbert.
>
> 19th July—Up betimes. Had a little re-adjustment of the shrouds seen to. Sailed in the evening for Ardrishaig and the North. Went into the canal at 9 p.m., mooring for the night above the first series of lochs. Started tow-

ing through at 6 o'clock next morning; arriving in Crinan Basin at 9.30 a.m. After breakfasting, and writing letters, ran out of canal and round to Crinan. Very wet and stormy.

21st July—Stormy and wet all day. Cleared up in the evening when sail was made for Loch Craignish. The scenery here was charming. Anchored in a pretty little bay at the north end of Righ Island. From this anchorage next day, a fine run with a stiff S.S.W. breeze took us to the Little Horse Shoe Bay, in Kerrera; by way of the Dorus Mhor, Pladda, Puilladobhrain and the Sound of Kerrera. It blew very hard all night and throughout the following day. Explored the ruins of Gylen Castle.

24th July—The weather has improved. Sailed to Oban and afterwards to Dunstaffnage, where another interesting old castle was visited. Next day we left Dunstaffnage and had a fine sail to Ardtornish in the Sound of Mull; afterwards running back to Oban, as my companion had to leave for the South.

27th July—I sailed single-handed for the Sound of Mull, anchoring for the night at Ardtornish, and going on the next day to Tobermory.

29th July—Heavy rain all night and best part of the day. Cleared up in evening so got under weigh at 7 p.m. and sailed with light breeze for Eigg. Becalmed for hours off Ardnamurchan. Picked up a breeze during the small hours. Weather became thick with heavy rain. Steered a compass course and ran into Eigg at 3 a.m.; day breaking.

30th July—Stiff N.W. breeze; glorious day. Sailed over to Arisaig under jib and mizzen and anchored in the lovely little Camus au Talmhuinn. Visited an old friend and stayed to supper. Perfect evening; glorious sunset, with the mountains of Rum and Skye in the distance. The next day was spent in taking a small party (plural) for a sail; returning in the evening, and going to dinner at the old house of Clanranald.

1st August—Left Arisaig and sailed along that magnificent stretch of mountainous coast which lies between that spot and Ardnamurchan point. Went into the wild and romantic Loch Moidart and anchored close to Castle Tirrim, the ancient home of the Clanranalds. Made a few sketches of the ruins, and explored the island of Reisger. Lovely moonlight night. Left next morning for Tobermory. Wind very light. Becalmed for hours off Ardmore and anchored at Tobermory at 3 a.m., after a long and latterly rather monotonous sail. Left Tobermory in the morning in company with a number of local boats bound for Loch Aline to take part in the Regatta. Stiff breeze; glass falling.

4th August—Loch Aline Regatta. Fresh gale blowing; some good sailing witnessed. Sailed next day for Oban. Had the usual afternoon calm, which made the day long. Spent a pleasant evening on board the *Raider*, Dr. and Mrs. Morris.

6th August—Went over to Oban for letters and received news that my future shipmate could not arrive in Oban before Wednesday; so decided to go south without delay. Sailed through Easdale and Cuan Sounds and anchored below Dog Castle in Torsa.

7th August—Made up my mind to go right through to Skipness in Loch Fyne. Raining when anchor was lifted at Torsa. Calm and quiet in the Dorus Mohr. Fine and sunny at Crinan. Fresh breeze at Ardrishaig which fell completely off Tarbert. Arrived at Skipness at Midnight, thus finishing the first part of Cruise. The rest of the month of August was spent in sketching and sailing round about Skipness, Loch Ranza, Inch Marnock, and Loch Fyne.

1st September—My relatives who had been spending August at Skipness departed for home; and after seeing them off I set sail for Tarbert to cruise in the company of *Quest II* and visit new anchorages with Messrs. Strange and Adderton.

Next day we sailed in company at 11 a.m., for Loch Gair; a place quite new to me. It is one of the most paintable spots on the coast, and many days were spent here; pleasant memories of which will long remain with me. While staying here Messrs. Strange and Adderton accompanied me in *Sheila* on a voyage of exploration to the upper waters of Loch Fyne. A fine morning with a light breeze saw us under weigh, and the weather continued good until half the return journey was accomplished, when down came the rain; and we finished the trip in the dark with no wind and a soaking deluge.

9th September—Both ships left for Tarbert; where in due course they arrived after a splendid sail in lovely weather.

11th September—Mr. Strange left for home and slavery (i.e., hard work), and on the 14th both *Quest II* and *Sheila* sailed for Loch Ranza where we stayed four days sketching.

19th September—Today saw us both back at Tarbert, and the 21st finished *Sheila*'s cruise. The total distance sailed from port to port was 540 nautical miles.

SHEILA crossing the Minch
by Robert Groves

In 1910 Albert Strange was to design another boat for his satisfied customer Groves; named *Sheila II* she was somewhat larger than her predecessor at just under 32 feet overall. Also in that year Strange designed another boat for himself, *Cherub III*, a 25 foot yawl with canoe counter stern, a design which personifies the canoe yawl as a type. Sadly she was sold soon after because of his failing health. *Cherub III* survives today, now renamed *Redwing*, and another boat *Emerald* was later built to the design.

5 Lean Times

MANY CANOE YAWLS, along with other Victorian and Edwardian boats, laid up in 1914 had no-one after the Great War fit or inclined to use them, and they quietly decayed away; but perhaps the scarcity of the remainder contributed to their desirability and ultimately their survival. Those boats fortunate enough to have survived the catastrophe have become icons of a former time.

Although a time of profound social change, the inter war years were too short and economically unstable to permit a renaissance of affordable leisure boating to any marked degree. The post-war shortage of men and materials was soon followed by the Wall Street Crash and the Great Depression. What we did begin to see at this time were changes in the design and construction of recreational craft through improvements in knowledge and, more especially, materials and engineering advances arising from wartime development. The war created a shift of commercial emphasis from individual craftsmanship to large scale manufacturing, and from natural materials to synthetics.

One of the earliest examples of modern synthetic materials in recreational craft about this time was the use of linoleum as a waterproof deck covering, and more were to follow. Most of the cruising boats built during this period were little changed in terms of design and construction from their pre war cousins but they did benefit greatly from wartime engine developments, and auxiliary engines became more common, along with increasing standards of interior comfort as better equipment and materials became available.

But the canoe yawl fell into decline, partly due to the death of Albert Strange in 1917, although George Holmes and a couple of others did continue to design them well into the late 1930s when the type went completely into the doldrums—where it remained until recent times. A number of boats were built to older canoe yawl designs in the early post war years and several of them survive to this day. These include *Nirvana* and several transom stern and canoe counter versions of Strange's own canoe yawl *Cherub III*.

In 1905 G. McLean Gibson had entered a canoe yawl *Gull* as his first attempt at yacht design in a Humber Yawl Club competition, where she was awarded first prize; however it has to be said that there were only two entries. The judge was Albert Strange and he commented that:

> "The drawing shows a powerful though easy rising mid-section carried fore and aft by harmonious buttock and bowlines; the whole body, both above and below water, being very consistent in idea and execution. There is ample cabin room, with a berth forward of the mast, though the bulkheads seem unnecessary, unless a 'paid hand' is carried, a thing hitherto unknown on a Humber Yawl. The ballast is given as totalling 1770 lbs., but if the boat were built of ordinary scantling, at least another 500 lbs. would be required which might easily be carried in the keel if it were made wider. As shown it is only 4in. siding amidships, and it might well be 6in. for the greater part of its length. The freeboard strikes one as being rather low, but the great height of deck crown to some extent obviates this defect. A handsome sail plan divided into three pieces ought to drive the boat well, especially to windward.

In 1923 the design was tinkered with, and the through deck centre plate was modified to fit within the accommodation, which enabled the cabin to be lengthened. *Alathea*, as she was named, was built by Abeking & Rasmussen in Germany. Some time later the design was resurrected as the Clyde Canoe Club One Design and three further boats were built in 1934. *Morag* survives today, and renamed *Mingulay* she awaits restoration on Humberside. As far as I know *Alathea* rotted away in the 1970s and *Ailie* was destroyed by fire. *Minna* survived until at least a few years ago.

There follows a short cruise account written by Edward Hicks Oliver, who bought the pretty little canoe yawl *Eel*, designed and built in 1896 by George Holmes for his

CLYDE CC ONE DESIGN, early 1930s

Derived from G McLean Gibson's GULL; 25ft x 22ft x 7ft 7in.

own use, around 1912. He also shared Holmes' love of sketching and his drawings clearly show a natural artistic talent. The account was first published in the Humber Yawl Club *Yearbook* of 1925. It well illustrates the severe weather that these plucky little ships could withstand, albeit the mizzen succumbed to the elements—but she was after all some 30 years old at the time. Hicks Oliver sold her in 1933 and she survives today, having recently emerged from restoration.

> "After a hot and uncomfortable journey from London to Tonbridge, it was a great relief to leave the stuffy train at East Farleigh, cross the level crossing and find ourselves once more on the narrow little stone bridge looking down at the old *Eel* lying against Coppen's float, where we had rigged her a week or two before. The Medway here is absurdly narrow and we had always seen it looking most placid, but to our great surprise it was now in full flood and there was such turmoil at the weir that it would have been folly to have tried to take a sailing boat past it. In fact, Coppen had sent me a wire, it appeared, warning me of the state of the river and hinting that I should not come down but, fortunately, I did not receive this wire until I returned home some days after. The lock-keeper had five or six sluices open and the water was consequently making a great fuss below the lock where it struck obliquely across the river onto a bank of concrete blocks, many of which were just below the surface.
>
> Next morning the water had dropped about a couple of feet and things looked much more promising. Coppen said he would help us out, and he and his son took a line to the left bank while we were in the lock, and as soon as the lock gates opened we pointed the *Eel* to the weir, which was on the right bank.
>
> On getting through the lock I realised that Coppen was, of course, right, as the *Eel* would have turned completely round were it not for his line pulling us down stream all the time. In two or three minutes it was all over and we had cast off and were drifting fast down the river. We found even now the *Eel* had a strong tendency to turn round, and to keep her straight it was

necessary to tow from the dinghy. We made good progress and by the time we had reached Maidstone the stream was running at its normal pace. We arrived at Allington lock by lunch time, a beautiful hot day with hardly a breath of wind. *Meander*, a smart motor yacht which had passed through Farleigh lock just before we did, was here waiting for water. A small motor yawl came along and offered to give us a pluck.

'To Chatham?' I asked.

'Yes, come along,' they replied, so we quickly hitched on. This sporting little boat gave us a nice, gentle passage, and on arriving at Chatham and hearing I was bound for Ockham Woods, they said they might as well go on there too and told us not to cast off. About 8.30, therefore, found us comfortably anchored off the woods, quite a long journey from Farleigh, especially in view of the obstacles, delays, and the late time of starting.

The wind rose in the night and in the morning we found ourselves on a lee shore, the wind blowing hard from the S.W. After breakfast I thought we had better get out, so under jib and mizzen, about as much as she could stand, we carried on down the river. At 11.00 we found ourselves at Queenborough among a crowd of other boats all sheltering, and during the day many others came in from Erith or Gravesend, all very snugly reefed and seemingly very glad to get in. Here Claud Wellard came over to call on us and invited us to later on have a look at his new purchase, a boat from Mersea, previously owned by Major J. Harden. She seemed very roomy and comfortable down below where Mrs. Wellard gave us a most generous and enjoyable tea. During the afternoon, in addition to the hard wind, we were treated to very bad rain squalls, hail and thunder. Wellard, however, seemed very optimistic about the weather, saying the glass was very high and that he was sure we should have an improvement next day.

We turned out at 6.30 the following morning, sky certainly more serene, but plenty of wind from the S.W. Still I thought we had better get our passage to the Crouch over before it got worse, so putting a reef in the mainsail, made a start. There was quite enough sea for us outside, especially off the Nore, but we made good progress and ticked off the measured mile in eight

Ernest Hicks Oliver's cruise in EEL

minutes. By 9.30 we had rounded the Whitaker beacon and then began the beat against wind and tide to the Crouch. Approaching the Crouch things began to get more interesting. The 12-metres were the first craft we saw in the distance, *Vanity*, *Atalanta*, and *Noreen*, and beautiful they looked with what seemed to us full sail set (although it turned out afterwards that this was not really so) and apparently disregarding the threatened squalls coming up from windward. As Wellard had predicted, however, the day improved as it got on and, after anchoring at the mouth of the river at about two o'clock for lunch and a shave, we had a most enjoyable sail up to Burnham, where we arrived at 5.30.

Saturday, 21st June—Went down to Burnham again. Most lovely afternoon and evening. Did not get under way, however, as many stores had to be purchased, and also one of the party could not get down till later in the evening. Mr. H. A. Tonge came alongside about eight o'clock and insisted on our going aboard and inspecting his new purchase *Dorothy May*. It was midnight before we returned to the *Eel*.

The next day was lovely, too, wind N.W., N. to E., light at first then fresh. We took the first of the ebb out of the Crouch and arriving at the W. Buxey buoy had a beat all the afternoon against the flood and the wind. It seemed almost impossible to get past the Buxey beacon, and at last at 3.30 we anchored well inshore, the wind having fallen very light. A little yawl flying the Blackwater S.C. burgee, which had been going about more or less with us gave up the attempt and returned to the Crouch. About four o'clock a fresh easterly breeze sprang up and we then got under way again. We were very close in, however, and we hadn't proceeded far before we saw right in front of us a large bank of sand. We went about very quickly and worked out for another mile or so. This easterly breeze was just what we wanted though, and when we were once away from the sand it took us at a great pace round Sales Point and into the little haven of Bradwell.

This little place, Bradwell Quay, had not changed at all, we were glad to find, since we were last here two years ago, in fact, it really has not changed much, apparently, for the last two or three hundred years. It is a most delightful little harbour, but as I have many times described this snug little place I ought not now to say any more about it. For a boat of the. *Eel*'s draught it is simply perfect and the fact that the entrance almost dries out at L.W.S. only makes the place more interesting. Sometimes one has to make a before-breakfast start to get out; at other times we quanted out, and the entrance is rather tortuous too. But, as I say, these characteristics only add interest to this little spot.

We made this our headquarters for a few days and took short cruises to the adjacent ports. One day we revisited Mersea and found the anchorage more crowded than ever. Going in we were led by a small single-hander which was apparently 'manned' by a red-headed boy in jersey and ex-white unmentionables, but on seeing this little craft later at anchor we found that the owner of the red hair was one of the fair sex, and we learnt that she was the original of a very charming portrait in the previous year's Academy by McBey. A visit another day to Wyvenhoe was memorable in that we missed our tide on the return journey some distance outside Bradwell, and I had a very hot and fatiguing tow from the dinghy to get her up the creek to our usual anchorage.

Sunday, 3rd August—Got out of creek about two hours before high water. Wind N.W. strong. Ran out to Bench Head, followed by two or three Mersea yachts. Two shaped their course for Harwich; whither we decided to go too. Much rough water off Colne Bar and unpleasant crossing Dovercourt Bay. It is very interesting passing the little watering places on this stretch of coast and noticing the difference in style of each. Between Frinton and Walton we were much amused at the appearance of the cliffs, which look for all the world like the made-up scenery of a Scenic Railway. Arrived at Harwich about 4.00, and the wind lightening had long beat up Orwell to Pin Mill, where we anchored at a little after seven o'clock. On the way up the river we picked up and passed a sailing barge, which rather pleased us, also saw at anchor the *Ultimus*, an enlarged *Eel* with a motor, built by Frank Maynard of Chiswick. Found the anchorage very crowded and were not impressed with Pin Mill as a Bank Holiday resort. Slept well, however, in spite of a chilly, threatening, cheerless evening, gramophones, and midnight revellers noisily enquiring for more beer.

Monday, 4th August—Got up at 6.00. Drizzle, and wind N.W. A little grey boat next to us said she was going to Brightlingsea, but we did not see her after leaving. Ran down the river and spoke *Ultimus* She said she was going to Maldon, but we did not see her again, either, after this. It was rough again crossing Dovercourt Bay, but once under the high land at Walton and along the coast we had a comfortable time. Held our tack till we got to the Bar Buoy, where we again found things bad for us and we had a wet time beating up the Blackwater. In going about near the Bench Head buoy the mizzen, after one or two warning squeaks, went by the board, but we managed to save the sail and the broken mast. Arrived at Bradwell about 1.15, tired after a hard sail.

Tuesday, 8th August—Got up at 5.30, dropped out of creek and anchored outside for breakfast. About 9.30 got under way with two reefs in the mainsail and with no mizzen, of course. Hard N.W'ly. Wind and rough water. A very damp beat up the Blackwater, but all went well until we got to Stangate, [this would have been Stansgate, Stangate being on the Medway—Ed] when the reef pennant parted. Anchored to put matters right and took the opportunity to have a sip of something and a piece of cake to help us on our way. Arrived outside the lock at Heybridge at 3.30, and had the satisfaction of knowing that we were one of the very few craft in this district which had been under way this disagreeable day.

With the exception of a week-end or two, this was about all we did this year, but after hearing other people's stories, I don't think we were as unfortunate as most during the wet and boisterous season of 1924.

In 1928 Uffa Fox designed the landmark *Avenger*; it had an innovative V-shaped hull which cut through the water and led to the modern racing dinghy as we know it today. Always innovative, he was also a keen canoeist and member of the Humber Yawl Club. Along with Roger de Quincy, a member of the Royal Canoe Club, he challenged for the New York Canoe Club International Trophy in 1933. Sailing sister boats, conforming to both the RCC 'B' Class rule and the American Canoe Association rule, they swept the board, taking the prestigious Seawanaka Cup.

He also crossed the channel to Cherbourg in *Brynhild*, a two-man sliding seat canoe, with his chief draughtsman in only 12 hours, and subsequently cruised along the North Brittany coast. He also crossed a very windy North Sea in *Vigilant*, an extreme light displacement 22 square metre, to Sweden and back without mishap. With a number of designs to his credit *Stardust* is perhaps one of the less well known. Her details were published in the *Yachting Monthly* of April 1940 and she was designed for an owner in Bombay. She is one of the very few modern examples of the earlier Victorian and Edwardian canoe yawls, even with the more modern fashion of Bermuda rig she is a pretty ship, spoilt only, we may think, by the doghouse.

Betsy was designed by W. Easton of West Mersea in 1930; one of several canoe counter yachts designed by him for a Colonel Blewitt, the father of Mary Blewitt, author of *Celestical Navigation for Yachtsmen*. *Betsy* was built by Walter Cook & Son at Maldon—unusually, for she was one of very few pleasure craft built in what was primarily a commercial yard. Perhaps there was a shortage of commercial work during the depression. She has been cruised fairly extensively and survives to this day.

Maurice Griffiths was brought up in Ipswich, where he was introduced to the maritime world, and a tour round an early steamship made a lasting impression on him. He left school in 1918 and took a job with an auctioneer and estate agent. In 1921, after a cruise on the Norfolk Broads, he bought his first boat, selling his model railway to pay for her. His love of boats now, apparently, exceeding his love of trains. When he lost his job two years later he started up his own yacht agency and the business prospered.

His regular cruising eventually led him into yacht design, alonside his other talents as yachting journalist & editor, writer and artist. As a naval officer he was awarded the George Medal for WW-II mine clearance work. As a yacht designer he advocated shoal draught and was familiar with the work of Albert Strange, which he admired, and which in later years inspired him to design a canoe yawl *Tamaris* for his own use,

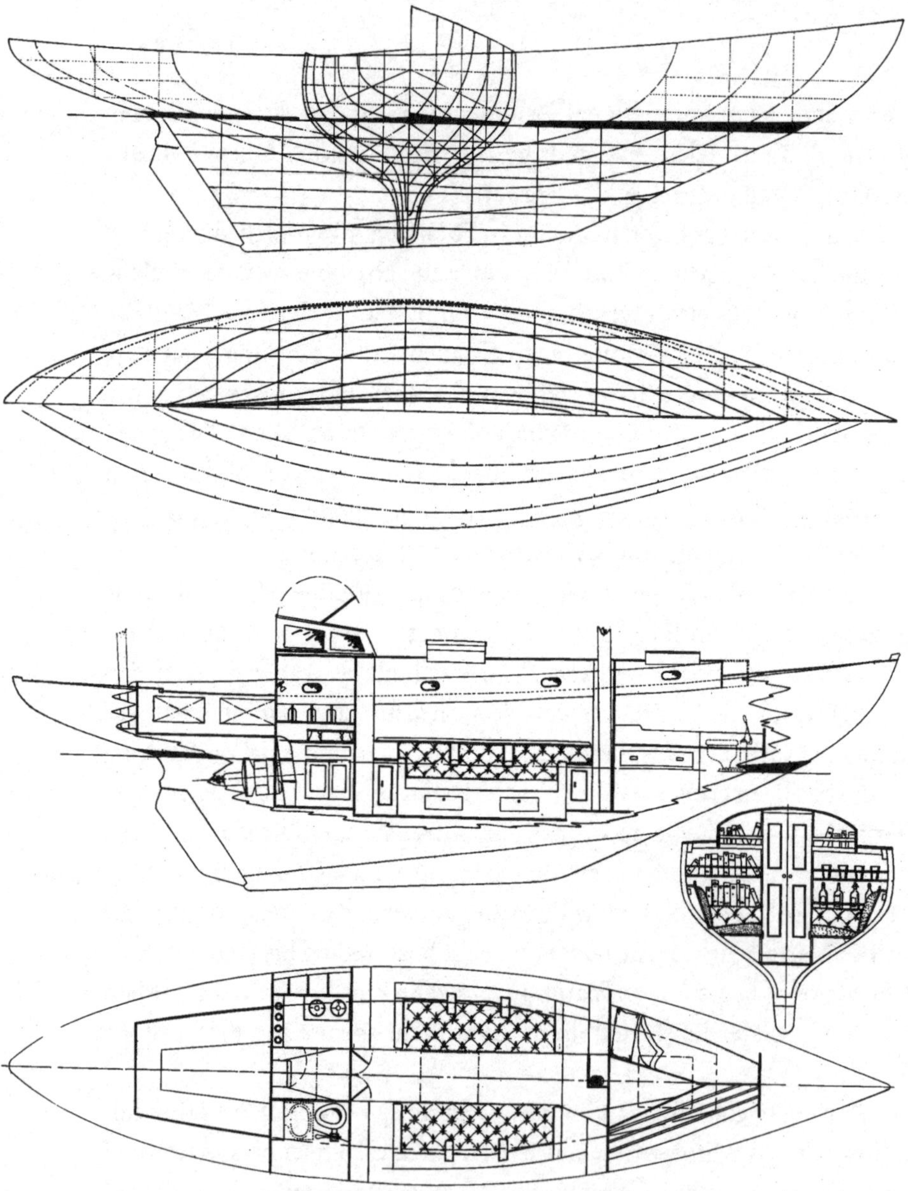

STARDUST, 1939

by Uffa Fox; 35ft x 25ft x 8ft 4in x 5ft, displacing 5.8 tons, sail area 647 sq ft. The overhangs eliminate the need for a bowsprit or bumkin.

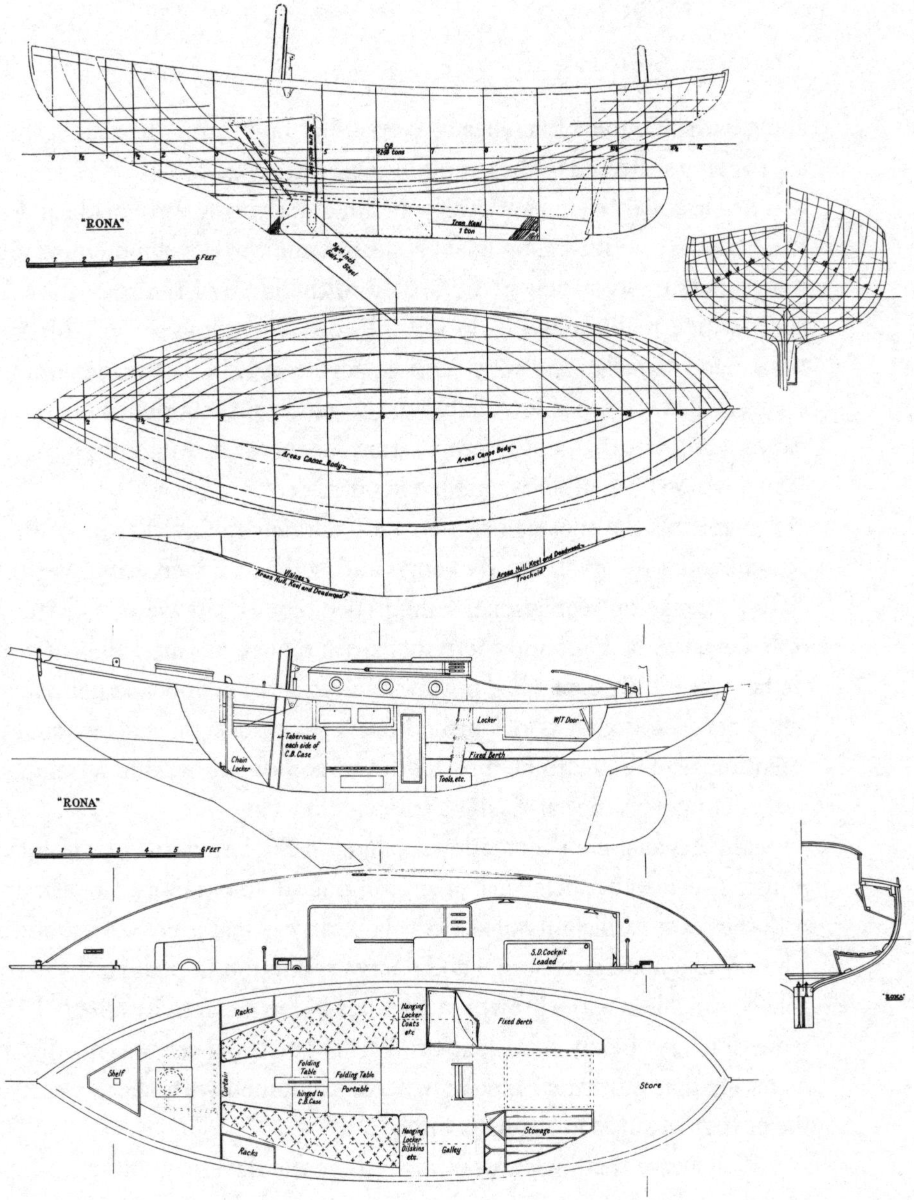

RONA, 1930

by W Easton, similar to BETSY; 24ft x 18ft x 7ft x 3ft, displacing 2,56 tons, sail area 333 sq ft. Designed for Easton's own use, built in the Phillipines and shipped to Burnham on Crouch for finishing.

along with a couple of ketches with a similar hull form. He died at the age of 90, his ashes being scattered in the sea off his beloved Essex coast.

Some advances in boat design and manufacturing were made and in yacht racing the J Class America's Cup boats appeared and the development of much faster and more reliable motor powered craft led to the birth of the recreational powerboat, a sport which really took off during the 1920's. Although some further refinements were made in design and construction, particularly in the smaller racing classes, once recovery had started it soon faltered, the gathering war clouds resulted in a preoccupation with re-armament in preparation for the next round of global conflict. World War II was to be another watershed in our story.

After this the shortage of men and materials followed as in WW1 and was again accompanied by great social change and with ever increasing wealth more people started to take up recreational sailing. The older boats were restored and some new ones began to be built and there was a resurgence of ships lifeboat conversions, but timber was tightly controlled post war and in short supply and hence expensive. Inevitably because the costs of finished boats were so high that few could afford them, attention again came to be directed towards more affordable boats, just as it had 80 years before with the early sailing and paddling canoes.

The expansion of recreational sailing in the latter half of the 19th Century was primarily driven by social change, new money, to use a more modern phrase, coupled with the ready availability of skilled labour at reasonable cost. All that was needed was a bit of imagination in design and a large reduction in boat size and you had affordable boating, hence the growth in all types of leisure activity afloat. This time, as size reduction had already been done pre WW1 something else was needed and it was new materials that motivated the change and combined with cheap construction fuelled the next great surge in leisure boating.

Well aware that high costs were stifling the development of sailing the Yachting Magazines started to offer plans and instructions for home building. These off the shelf plans did away with the need for a bespoke design which was to prove a significant cost saving.

The *Yachting Monthly* 3-Tonner, designed by Alan Buchanan and which appeared in 1946 is a good such example, and was considered at the time as an ideal design for the amateur. Traditionally built the construction was simplified by a complete lack of reverse curves in the sections leaving a large deadwood section which was not planked over. The coach roof extends right to the topsides, and although this meant a little difficulty with the moulds in that vicinity, much material and labour were saved.

Traditional boat building in wood is however a skilled job and is time consuming, making for an expensive commodity. The labour costs can be as much as 75 or 80% of the total, which has remained the case from the end of the Great War, up to the present day. Another early design was the *Yachting World* Cadet which was designed by Jack Holt, cheap and simple to construct it was really a class racing dinghy in miniature, the boat handled well and was followed by many similar designs over the years.

One of the major advances in materials which came out of WW2 developments was the improvement in waterproof glues which led directly to the production of marine plywood which was to revolutionise recreational boatbuilding, a process helped by men and women who had become skilled in its use as a construction material for boats and aircraft entering the commercial labour market. This particular development led to a reduction in labour costs to about 60% of the total build, but another even more revolutionary idea was about to emerge.

Subsequent relaxations on timber controls led to the next stage of cheap home building and was based upon wartime experience of prefabrication, this was the advent of the 'kit boat' with pre cut plywood panels and pre-machined timber strips. These were marketed more cheaply than it was possible at the time to buy the timber and plywood separately from a merchant. They could also be built in half the time and such were the advantages in time and money professional builders started to order kits and supply part finished and complete boats.

One by one other designs suitable for prefabrication followed, though these were still limited to the most popular in view of the cost of the initial precision jigs to machine the plywood sheets. The most famous and numerous by far of all kit boats was the ubiquitous *Mirror* dinghy which came much later, designed by Jack Holt and Barry Bucknell in 1962. It was sponsored by the 'Daily Mirror' and has sold over 70,000 to date and has served as an introduction to building and sailing for an enormous number of people, myself included.

The age of do-it-yourself boatbuilding had begun and the Bell Woodworking Company was to the fore, as well as the Mirror dinghy they produced a full range of kits for various designs of tenders, dinghies, motor craft and yachts. One of these was the Seagull Sloop, 18' 6" overall with a retractable keel, designed for coastal, estuary and inland cruising by Ian Proctor. She had a round bilge formed from butt jointed plywood planking; the kit also included separate packs of fastenings, fittings, paints and sails, even a choice of covers, trailer and outboard were supplied extras.

Although a similar, larger version, the 'Seamew Sloop' was also produced for the most part post WW2 cruiser designs in wood migrated from these round bilge hull forms to single or double chine. With only two or three planks per side respectively they are obviously not at all practical for a Canoe Hull and this contributed further to the decline of the type.

Multi chine 'stitch and tape' construction did enable some new canoe designs to be offered and easily built but it was when edge glued timber, now generally known as 'strip plank' became a reliable method of construction primarily due to better adhesives, especially epoxies, became available economic one-off round bilge construction become a reality. This provides a brand new window of opportunity for the canoe yawl because the fundamental problem when building a canoe hull is the large amount of twist in the planks at the ends which are quite fine and strip planking solved this problem at a stroke.

The other cost saving method of construction which developed after the Second World War was glass reinforced polyester whereby, briefly, glass cloth is draped around a mould also known as a 'plug', and impregnated with polyester resin and finished smooth with a gel coat. This is then fitted with a deck made in a similar manner and the two halves bonded together and it is then fitted out. As a manufacturing process it requires less skill and reduces the labour content but needs a substantial original investment to make the mould, hence a number of boats have to be built in order to break even.

Relative affluence has returned once more but I, and indeed many others, consider what is preventing younger sailors taking up boating as a hobby is the lack of affordable boats, berths and storage and nowadays the average age of members at most sailing clubs is increasing year on year. The only alternative for many at entry level cruising is an elderly, sometimes poorly designed GRP boat. One of these can cost less than the annual charges for some marina berths and unlike wooden ones which decay away if unloved, these things go on forever. What is needed is a particularly virulent mutation of osmosis to rid us of these abominations and stimulate some new and original thinking about entry level boats.

6 Some Design Basics

I HOPE TO CONVEY HERE something of the art and science of yacht design which underpins my belief that the canoe yawl is the ideal small cruising boat. My aim is not 'how to design a Yacht'—there are better publications on that subject than ever I could write—it is just to discuss pertinent technical aspects, past and present, in as readable a manner as possible.

Crude though some of the early examples may appear to modern eyes, their basis was mostly sound, and some, if not most of them, remain relevant today, a testament to ther designers who worked in relative isolation, without the ready access to information which we take for granted today.

A common expression is that if it looks right then it most likely is. A good example would be the Clipper ships and the J-class racers, amongst the most memorable and admired examples of sailing boat design; combining beauty and elegance with performance and functionality. The canoe yawl rates alongside them as an equal, its credentials are impeccable; it looks right and it is a beautiful example of a recreational sailing craft. Its sailing and sea keeping qualities are the stuff of legend; the original boats made notable passages in atrocious conditions in spite of their size.

The modern trend for supplementary systems to ensure fitness for purpose is to me an indication of poor design. In addition the current fashion for insurance-backed risk assessment, rather than sound professional judgment, can also undermine safety. A risk of once in 100 years does not mean that it cannot happen in year one. I would not wish to convey the impression that I consider modern design to be bad, which it certainly is not, and much of it is quite exceptional indeed; rather that it is not necessarily always good, and there is much that can be learnt from the past.

Most desirable characteristics in sailing craft are mutually contradictory, therefore a good design balances one against the other to produce an overall compromise to suit the type of sailing intended, to make the boat a pleasure to sail, a joy to her owner and a delight to the eye of the world. I will now try to explain the principles involved without resorting to unnecessary complications of terminology or an excess of mathematics or science. The more complex matters have of necessity been simplified; this is a story not a textbook after all.

Scott Russell's wave form theory along with the further development work by Colin Archer and Albert Strange have all been discarded, Harrison Butler's work on Admiral Turner's metacentric shelf theory shared a similar fate. Whilst there is a hydrodynamics case to be made against wave form theory there is no doubt that Colin Archer produced exceptionally seaworthy boats, as did Albert Strange, and it cannot be denied that many boats built in accordance with Turner's theory are remarkably steady on their course.

All these theories were attempts to produce a balanced hull form and in this sense they are still relevant today. A balanced hull form is one where the fore and aft underwater sections are more or less equal in volume and the curve of the rate of increase in volume from the bow to the midsection and reduction back to the stern are carefully defined. They will also remain fairly level without undue movement in or out of the water at the bow or stern when heeled; Turner's theory was an attempt to refine this latter element even further.

Others have since put forward alternative theories, but there is still much that we do not yet, or perhaps may never, understand. I offer you some words on sailing craft by an exceptional designer, which I think sum it up rather nicely:

> “Scientifically, they present a problem so complex that a complete solution is out of the question... Above all, good reader, beware of him who claims knowledge of yacht design, for we know only about the rudiments, the rest is conjecture — *Jack Laurent Giles*

Rigs have probably changed more in the last century than other elements of sailing boat design due to the increase in knowledge of the science of aerodynamics and because of the advances in materials engineering. Improvements have been made in our understanding of the fundamentals of yacht design, for example our knowledge of seaworthiness has increased considerably since the 1979 Fastnet race.

Modern studies have confirmed some suspicions, long held by mariners, such as a boat being much less stable on the crest of a wave than in a trough and that some waves are bigger, occasionally very much so, than the average for the sea state at any one time. These have given modern designers the ability, though not always the inclination, to improve the performance of sailing craft without undermining safety, by enabling a better understanding of the magnitude and direction of forces acting upon the whole structure.

Many developments in yacht design stem, as in the past, from racing rules; and sadly the European Union's *Recreational Craft Directive* now appears to have put cruising yacht design into a straitjacket. The early yachts had more seaworthy hulls because they were based on pilot and revenue vessels which had evolved fitness for purpose and good manners over two centuries.

Marchaj carried out extensive work on capsize probability using the Fastnet race inquiry as a basis; he related form characteristics to capsize occurrence and found a very strong correlation between the two irrespective of boat size. The Fastnet disaster was extreme, but his work shows that the capsize probability for boats with excessive length/beam ratios is three times higher than for more moderate values; displacement/length ratios showed lighter boats with more than twice the risk of higher-displacement vessels, and a high tenderness ratio (an IOR factor penalising a low centre of gravity) was more than four times as likely to cause a capsize as a more conservative value.

The performance of any sailing boat is defined by individual design considerations; primary, that is of fundamental importance; secondary, less significant and incidental, with minor impact in proportion to the whole. These considerations vary considerably between cruisers and racers as the following table will illustrate. This might explain why expert racing sailors appear to me to come to grief more often than is the case with less competent cruising sailors. It also illustrates why I consider the concept 'cruiser/racer' a contradiction in terms.

	Racing	Notes	Cruising	Notes
Hull configuration				
Length	Primary	Limits speed	Incidental	Defines weight
Weight	Primary	Creates resistance	Secondary	Limits handling
Stability	Primary	Limits sail area	Primary	Reduces capsize risk
Form	Incidental	Least resistance	Primary	Defines sea-keeping
Keel selection				
Type	Incidental	Small impact	Secondary	Defines handling
Depth	Secondary	Increases speed	Incidental	Limits area of use
Drag	Incidental	Reduces speed	Incidental	Reduces speed
Sail plan				
Area	Secondary	Limited by hull	Primary	Depends on use
Height	Secondary	Reduces drag	Incidental	Increases heel
Type	Incidental	Lowest weight	Secondary	Easy handling

MAJOR DESIGN ELEMENTS
with regard to boat use

Length is critical in a racer—the longer the faster—but it impacts on weight which increases hull immersion and so resistance, and reduces speed. In a cruiser, length will improve seaworthiness but limits the ease of handling. Stability is the measure of a boat's ability to return to an upright position after heeling, and determines the amount of sail that can be carried without capsize. Both types need to stay right side, up but racers want maximum stiffness at the optimum angle of heel, cruisers a more moderate amount over a wider range.

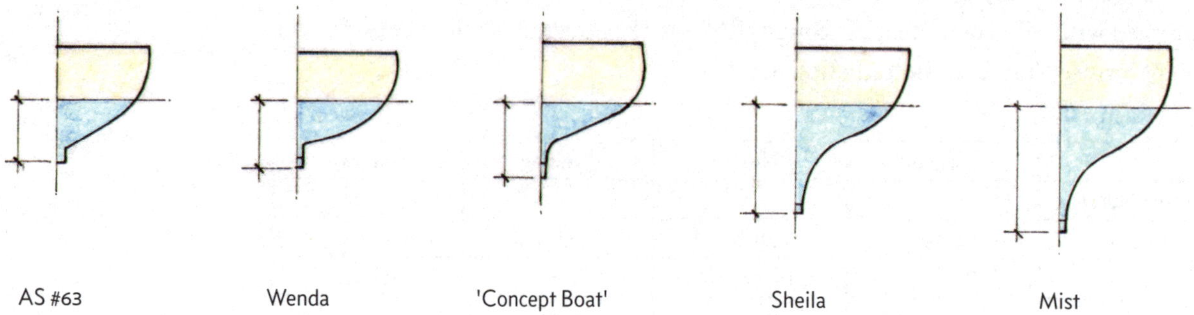

MID-SECTION: *Five hulls with similar waterline length but very different in section: Strange's No. 63 intended for the shallows of East and South Coast cruising, and the only one with a straight keel; Wenda for the Thames Estuary. My 'marina hopper' (see appendix) has a finer underwater shape, but on reflection I would increase her draught to 2ft 6in and dispense with the plate; Sheila was for the west coast of Scotland so somewhat deeper; finally Mist was designed for the Irish Sea and the Atlantic coast of Ireland, so deeper still. There is no 'one size fits all'.*

So we can now see that the hull is the key element in any boat; it dictates what is to be, and how it will be done. For a racer, form and keel type are minor considerations; but hull form is especially critical on a cruiser, the type of keel less so but both have considerable impact on the critical matter of sea-keeping ability.

Sail area and height on a racer are dictated by the weight and hydrodynamic characteristics of the hull, but for a cruiser increases in sail area or height add to the probability of capsize. Rig type is a lesser consideration with the racer, but not so with the cruiser, as sail handling is of fundamental importance.

The rating rules have spawned a new generation of cruisers which mimic many of the bad characteristics of the class racing craft, still primarily 'rule cheats' as they always have been, and the type has somewhat usurped traditional and more seaworthy designs. By exploiting the rules boats get a lower rating, the same overall effect as a speed advantage, but it rarely makes them better boats. The form characteristics are a fine long bow, large beam, full quarters, wide stern and a short deep fin keel with a dagger rudder, well aft.

This unbalanced hull form has been moderated a little in modern cruisers, but the form characteristics for the most part remain. This means a tendency to bury the bow into the waves when heeled as the broad stern quarter is lifted by virtue of its high volume relative to the immersed bow. In strong winds this causes her to slew into the wind and an alert helmsman is all that stands between order and chaos; when

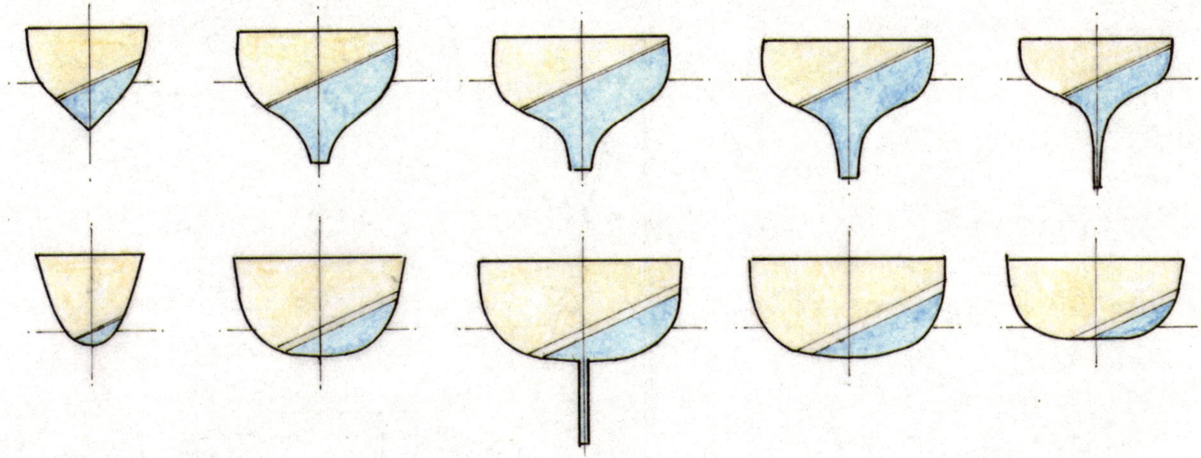

running before a strong wind the boat now slews from port to starboard inducing a rolling motion, and requires constant steering correction.

Traditional narrow, heavy displacement hulls have a low centre of gravity giving them *weight stability*, whereas wide-beamed light displacement hulls have a high CG, and rely more upon *form stability*. Traditional hulls heel easily initially then become increasingly resistant to further heeling, while the opposite is true of a racing hull: its form is very resistant to heeling initially, but much less resistant to further heeling. This characteristic of a hull form unbalanced in extreme conditions was the cause of the Fastnet disaster.

These hull characteristics cause the two types to behave in different ways when heeling, and when analysed they have two distinct components. The first of these, *static stability*, is the still-water state from which all measurements are carried out and is dictated by the weight and cross sectional shape of the hull. A static stability curve is then produced, plotting the magnitude of the righting lever against heel angles from 0° to 180°. Stability defines the ability to carry sail and its magnitude will dictate how much sail and in what conditions of weather, which is why traditional hulls forms are usually considered better for cruising boats.

HULL BALANCE: *Traditional and modern hull forms when heeled; the balanced tradition hull (top) shows a consistent rise above datum along its length, but the modern hull shows a clear imbalance between the fore and aft sections, explaing a tendency to bury the bow and lift the stern.*

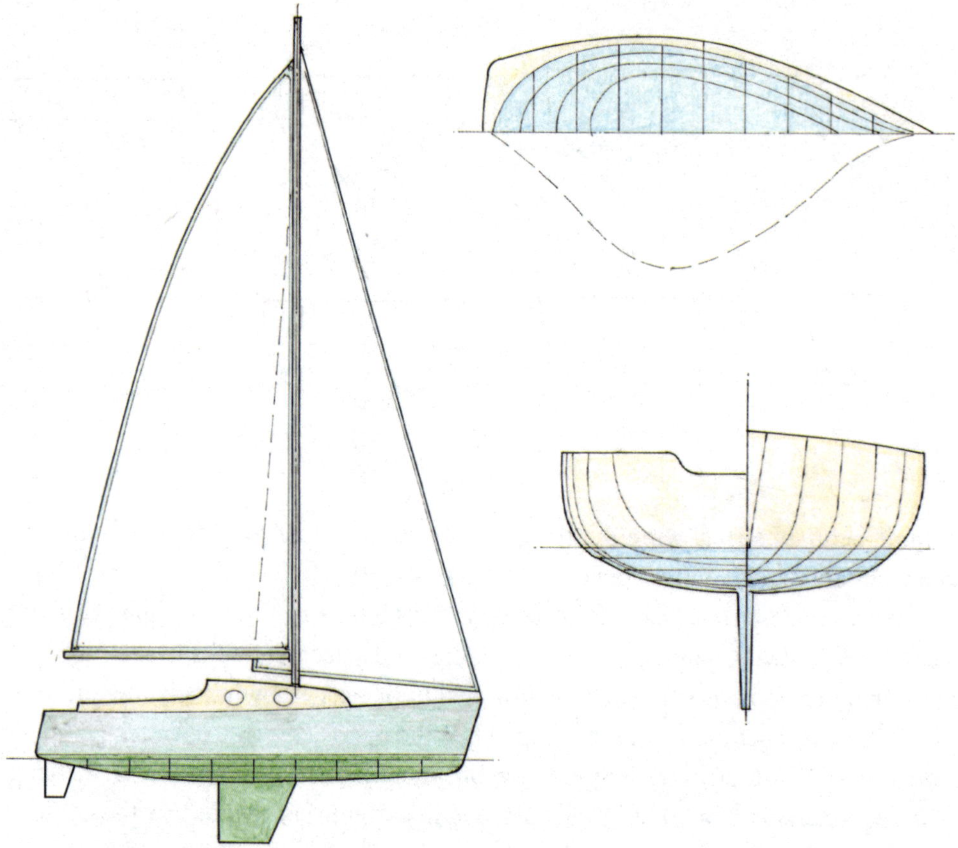

A MODERN SMALL CRUISER

Dynamic stability is determined by friction from the flow of water over the hull and wave generation on the water surface; the condition is complex and varies considerably. It is best illustrated by the simple example of a very small boat becoming far more stable once it is moving through the water. It can be a major component in smaller craft and the effect is known as damping; it reduces the degree and speed of the roll motion. The other components of damping are vortices generated by the hull and sails.

A traditional heavy displacement hull with a long keel will have more damping than a light displacement fin keel version. This is because of the higher lateral plane

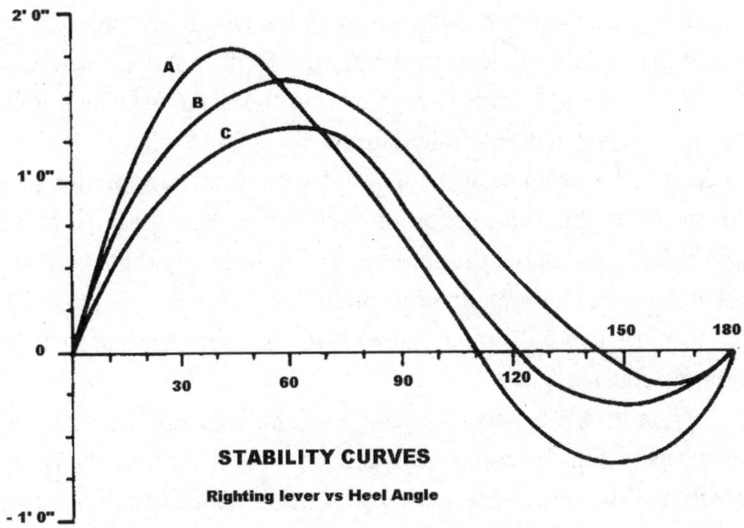

STABILITY CURVES:

A – Modern cruiser
B – 'Concept Boat' (see Appendix)
C – Wenda

A shows a boat intially stiff with a lrger maximum righting lever than the Canoe Yawls, but unfortunately it falls off steadily after 45 degrees, has a lower angle of vanishing stability and a longer range of negative stability than the other two. Of the two Canoe Yawls the firmer bilge and higher feeboard of the 'Concept Boat' have improved on both this angle and range. Interestingly, at the bottom end of a F5 (wind speed 17mph) both the modern cruiser and the Concept Boat have a similar angle of heel, due to the longer and lower sail plan of the Canoe Yawl.

of the former and, though to a lesser extent, a better cross sectional shape. The damping force generated by the sails is very considerable, for example when beating upwind the hull and sail forces are working together and the boat is exceptionally stiff, averaging only about 10° of heel. These forces diverge as the angle of wind increases and can lead to dynamic instability with some unbalanced hull forms and sail plans.

One important element of the static stability curve is the point where the boat becomes more likely to stay wrong side up, known as the *angle of vanishing stability* (A_{VS}) after which the boat needs a wave, perhaps a large one, to get it back right side up. The A_{VS} is not the only thing to consider: the slope of the curve, i.e., the rate of increase or decrease is equally important, as is the area under the curve which indicates work done. These are the elements which define the ease or otherwise by which a boat will either capsize or return to upright after inversion.

The curve can be useful in other respects when evaluated and tuned to enhance desirable characteristics. For example for a cruiser 20-30° of heel is about the optimum, so we would want a fairly steep slope up to this value and a steady progressive increase to a maximum somewhere between 45° & 60° (about the limit of human tolerance) followed by a long, slow decline to the A_{VS} and finally a short, shallow curve back to 180°. A number of typical curves are shown in the diagram, which indicates the marked differences between different hull forms.

The much quoted 'easy motion in a seaway' is another contradiction, what is easy for one sailor might be grim indeed for another. Again, balance must be the watchword, an easy rolling motion can induce sea sickness in some but undue stiffness, which causes extreme acceleration in movement, has a similar effect on others. Similarly traditional 'v' shaped hulls pitch more slowly in a seaway than their 'u' shaped light displacement cousins.

The interaction between the driving force of the sails and the hull is a complex one. The means by which the correct relationship is derived uses the *centre of effort* (CE) of the sails and the *centre of lateral resistance* (CLR) of the hull. An empirical or rule of thumb calculation, it is usually based on experience. The CE of the rig is the geometric centre of the sail area seen in profile; similarly the CLR is the geometric centre of the underwater area of the hull seen in profile; both of these vary with the disposition of the sails and the angle of heel.

Reefing causes the CE to move fore and aft, depending on the sail plan. The designed CE is always located in front of the CLR and this distance is called 'lead' and defines *helm balance*. By now you will not be surprised that this also varies, depending on the hull form. The true aerodynamic CE and hydrodynamic CLR are, incidentally, nowhere near their geometric counterparts. One thing that is fairly certain is unbalanced sail plans and hull forms will have more change in the position of the CE and the CLR when heeled, increasing *weather helm*.

Weather helm is the tendency of a boat to point further into the wind as she heels, due to changes in lead. This is desirable in small extent to give the rudder more 'grip' and the helm more 'feel', but when marked it results in physical demands on the helmsman in keeping the boat on course. A boat with some weather helm will, if left unattended, 'round up' into the wind and stop, which is a safety feature. Lee helm is the exact opposite of weather helm, being a tendency to point away from the wind when heeled, due to a decrease in lead, which is undesirable in any amount and highly dangerous in excess.

A good cruising hull is going to fall somewhere between the various extremes and not possess too much of anything. Exceptional weather conditions much above F6/F7 are rare for the average thinking sailor; he would experience them infrequently and a good balance seems to me appropriate. The only reasonable guarantee of safety is a truly seaworthy boat with the potential to survive extreme conditions if experienced. The ideal cruiser is the one which will, for the most part, sail herself, with the minimum amount of human intervention.

She would be well mannered and well balanced, with seaworthiness and ease of handling as the prime considerations in her design rather than dealt with as supplementary to the cramming of as much accommodation as possible into a given waterline length. With cruising sailing boats there is no 'one size fits all', she should be fit for the purpose her owner intends to put her to in the waters she is to sail.

7 Why the Canoe Yawl?

THE FIRST PART OF THIS BOOK is a narrative of the origins and development of the canoe yawl in all its variants, reflected against the background of other types of recreational craft. The last few chapters are more difficult to write as any appreciation of the type will inevitably include my opinions, personal preferences and prejudices and, on some occasions, intense dislike. Be reassured, however, that any dislike of mine is only directed at conformity, uniformity, restriction of choice and spurious legislation.

With the basics of yacht design covered in the previous chapter, let us consider the suitability of the canoe yawl as a type with respect to realistic likely use. Let us forsake the well-worn arguments about heavy or light displacement; gaff, lug or Bermudan rig; deep, long, short or drop keels; sloop, cutter, ketch or yawl, and concentrate instead, with an open mind, on fitness for purpose. A thorough evaluation has the potential to save the beginner, or even an experienced sailor, much trouble, expense and inconvenience.

Most people buy a boat to fulfil a dream, yet a lot of these dreams remain unfulfilled because of the difference between dream and reality. This is not to decry dreams, they are the stuff of progress; but dreams must be put to the test of logic before money is parted with. I am suggesting a hard-nosed assessment of need, practicality of handling, and the opportunities for use, to enable a better decision as to what boat should be acquired.

> “Human beings find it difficult in all spheres to base their opinions upon evidence, rather than upon their hopes — *Bertrand Russell*

Be realistic about the sort of sailing you are likely to do. Will you ever really sail much *en famille?* They may come once and never again. Is that worth the compromise of a capacious but poorly performing and over-equipped tub? The object of the exercise, I submit, is *pleasurable sailing* with sufficient but not excessive accommodation.

When considering hull volume think about onboard 'facilities'. It is worth remembering that nowadays it is not necessary to be self sufficient for a considerable length of time, given legs of short duration between marinas and other ports of call. A modest cost for an overnight berth will provide toilets, showers, washing machines, fresh water and electricity. Hot food will usually be available to supplement the shipboard menu. On board 'facilities' can be kept to a minimum using lightweight equipment and materials, without undue personal discomfort or restriction on the range and duration of cruises.

A single burner cooker with an integral cylinder is more than adequate for most needs; at breakfast time, make a sandwich lunch with a flask of soup and another of coffee. This can then be consumed whilst underway later in the day. Simplicity is the keyword, it can be regarded as comfortable camping afloat, it will mean less kit hence less expense, less to go wrong & less to fret about. This will considerably reduce the volume and cost of a suitable boat.

The next consideration is draught. Canoe yawls have been designed and built with deep keels, but given the modest beam the hull form is far more suited to shoal draught, with or without a plate. It is worth remembering that the deep-keeled *Sheila* draws only 3ft 4in and was designed to cruise the deep waters of the Western Isles which she did very successfully; shallow draught means a lighter and cheaper boat. A centre board will give access to places others cannot reach, allowing running up onto beach or mud, and perhaps dispensing with a dinghy.

The slim hull form of the canoe yawl reacts very quickly to a puff of wind, reaching hull speed faster than other forms, and it also is less impeded by a chop. For these reasons it will frequently outperform longer vessels which 'on paper' should be quicker. It has less, if any, need of a motor as sculls or a single sweep will have no problem moving it, albeit a little slower, when the wind drops. When sleeping aboard,

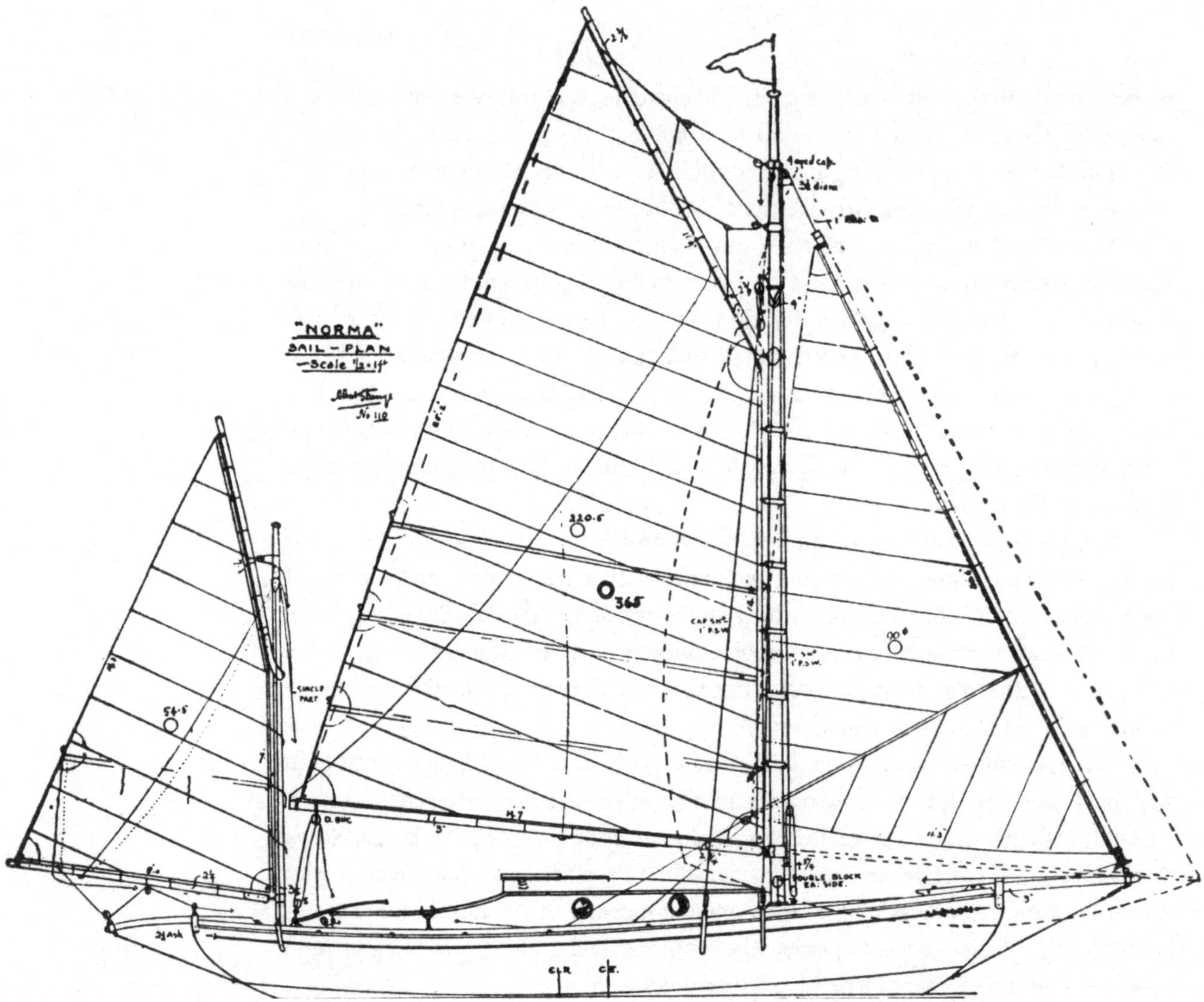

Why the Canoe Yawl? — **NORMA** *by Albert Strange, 1910*
25ft 5in x 20ft x 7ft 2in x 3ft 5in; sail area 365 sq ft; displacement 3.35 tons; ballast keel 1.33 tons.

Launched around 1914 and based for 7 years at Hoylake on the Wirral peninsula; acquired circa 1922 by a Captain Briercliffe who kept her for 18 years until she broke away from her moorings in the Menai Straits during a gale in 1940 and was lost. She has waited many years to be reincarnated.

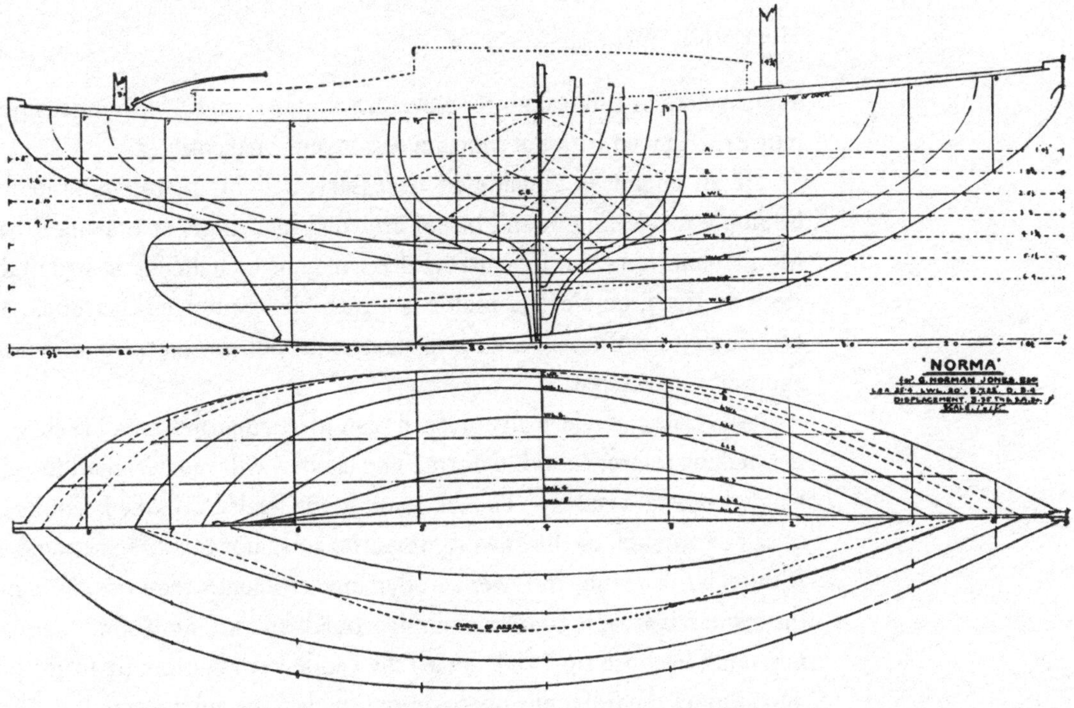

'NORMA'
for G. NORMAN JONES Esq.
DISPLACEMENT

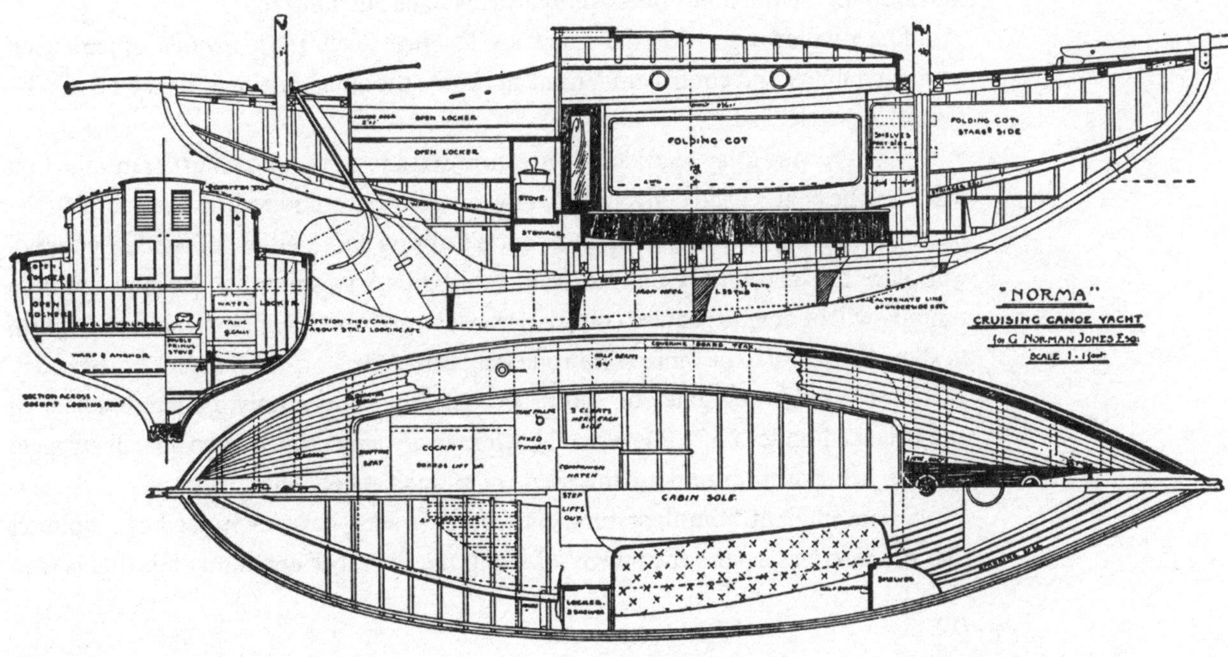

OPEN LOCKER
OPEN LOCKER
STOVE
STOWAGE
FOLDING COT
SHELVES
FOLDING COT STARB'D SIDE
WARP & ANCHOR
WATER TANK
COCKPIT
COMPANION HATCH
CABIN SOLE
SHELVES
"NORMA"
CRUISING CANOE YACHT
for G Norman Jones Esq.
SCALE 1 · 1foot

a canoe stern or canoe counter makes for a quieter night, without any of the wave slapping experienced with flat transom or conventional counter.

If an engine is considered necessary, a light quarter-mounted outboard will be ample for getting in and out of crowded moorings, or making it back to work by Monday morning. An inboard auxiliary may be a challenge to install due to the slim stern sections; an electric motor is a possible answer and batteries, low down, will contribute to stiffness. Nowadays electric propulsion units are increasingly available and well worth a look.

We cannot declare any one sail plan to be superior on all points of sailing without making reference to hull form. The canoe yawl was designed for short- or single-handed coastal cruising. The slim hull lends itself to, indeed requires, a low centre of sail effort such as the yawl rig imparts, so as not to suffer extreme angles of heel. Although this results in lower aerodynamic efficiency than the sloop or cutter rig for the same sail area, it confers a number of advantages not found together, sometimes not at all, in those rigs; this makes the canoe yawl supremely fit for purpose, taking into account the full range of conditions likely to be encountered.

The divided rig, with the mizzen's leverage well aft, provides unparalleled manoeuvrability and control under sail alone, for the small or single crew, and in relative calm or gale.

When getting away, particularly in a crowded anchorage, hoisting the mizzen first will hold the boat's head conveniently to wind as long as required, and on slipping the mooring, holding the mizzen briefly to one side by its boom—the 'air rudder' effect—will place the boat on the desired tack with ease. (A strong cross- or opposing tide running will of course require consideration, for example the plate would be kept up to allow the vessel to be more wind-rode than tide-rode.)

Even in a bit of a gale you can proceed safely, snugly, only moderately heeled, and balanced under jib & mizzen only, while many single-masted boats will struggle through being over- or under-canvassed, or of unbalanced helm.

Some eminent commentators, past and present have expressed the opinion that the mizzen has an 'advantage' of being the first reef in a blow; but this is true only of beamy, unbalanced hulls which develop excessive weather helm when they heel, and the practice discards all the principal advantages which the yawl has to offer. To earn its keep, the mizzen must be a substantial sail, around 15% of the total area for cruising. It should be the first sail up and the last down so that when in use with the jib and without the mainsail the rig is balanced. With a moderate sail area there should be no need for reefing on either the jib or mizzen unless in very heavy weather.

For greater speed the mizzen can be increased up to around 25% of the total area, with a reef point back to 15%, but now the jib, the powerhouse, will be larger and with roller reefing, to balance the two settings on the mizzen, and will exceed the mizzen in area when conditions are right. All this costs more money of course, but it illustrates the supreme adaptability of the canoe yawl; true, it will never beat a racer 'around the cans', but it will show a clean pair of heels to almost any cruiser of similar size, without dipping you in the water in the process.

To its ease of balancing we can add further advantages of the yawl rig: the mainmast is stepped further forward, providing greater accommodation space amidships; a centre plate, where fitted, can be further forward also, which will reduce the degree of weather helm when the boat is heeled, making her easier to steer; in some designs the shorter boom may stop short of the cockpit, reducing risk of a crack on the head, which is certainly not the case with sloops and cutters.

With a balanced hull and rig the well-designed canoe yawl sails beautifully, requiring minimal attention to rudder and sail trim when compared to other types. It was well-conceived in a range of sizes, and keel and hull forms, to suit local conditions; it has been honed to perfection over the years. This is why I consider it to be as near to the ideal small cruiser as anything yet produced.

One of the great pleasures of sailing is social contact with like-minded and like-boated people; here the canoe yawl wins hands-down over a production boat, and it also looks and feels a lot better. Our Victorian forbears had to be self-reliant sailors and the truly thoroughbred canoe yawl was sculpted by the prevailing conditions to meet their needs admirably.

8 Some Notable Survivors

THAT THERE ARE ANY SURVIVORS, let alone some still sailing, from the heyday of the canoe yawl is remarkable. Some are now centenarians, and all have endured both care and neglect by successive owners over the years; rot, recession and two World Wars have contributed to their difficulties. Some have been restored and are lovingly cared for; others have been bought but await restoration and others are still sadly neglected. The search for survivors continues.

Here are the stories of seven of our 'rare breed'. They range from centenarians of 118 years old to mere youngsters of 86. Some other survivors have been included in the main text either because of their pivotal role in the development of the type or just a scarcity of suitable examples for that particular period in time. Where this has been done I have tried to expand the content relating to them in order to do them the justice they deserve.

Lucky Star of 1893 is a venerable lady at 18ft × 5ft 3in beam, built by Turk at Kingston on Thames and based at Burnham on Crouch. Her history is sketchy but she is truly remarkable both for her condition and the extent of the remaining original construction. She was truly born under a lucky star and was beautifully restored by Fabian Bush of Rowhedge in 1996, who incidentally also built *Constance* to Strange's *Wenda* design, described later. Lucky Star is a pristine example of a Victorian canoe yawl, and she is in very good hands.

Her provenance remains a mystery; she was originally thought to have been an ex-police sailing launch, but the curator of the Police Museum has cast doubts on this; research on her origins continue. The earliest traceable owner was Roger Hadlee, owner of the Royal Exchange Art Gallery, who bought her via *Exchange and Mart* in

LUCKY STAR
18ft × 5ft 3in

1976. All that is known is her previous owners lived in Paddock Wood in Kent and sailed the boat at Cuxton on the River Medway. She was later sold to Oliver Swan of the Tyron and Swan Marine Art Gallery, and laid in his barn until uncovered by her present owner Ant Law.

She was hogged, her back broken, and the seller insisted that if she fell in half on the journey to her new home he would not be held responsible. In fact she survived the journey intact; unfortunately the road trailer did just that, falling in half on the way home. Her restoration was carried out retaining as much of her original structure as possible, the keel was reinforced, the transverse floors replaced and the planking was refastened up to the waterline and at the ends where it had sprung away. She retains her original Victorian fittings. She sails regularly, cruising from Burnham round the Isle of Sheppey and into the Medway and back, to West Mersea and Pin Mill, and to every nook and cranny in the Rivers Crouch and Blackwater.

Eel of 1895, mentioned earlier, was designed by George Holmes for his own use and built by J.A. Akester at Hornsea. Holmes cruised in her extensively during his 17 years of ownership, including shipping her by steamer to Germany, Belgium and Holland. The first part of her history is well documented but her story in recent years is perhaps less well known. The man who saved her was Alan Staley, a boatbuilder at Faversham. He first met her in 1964 when she parted her mooring in Whitstable Bay and, fortuitously, blew ashore on the end of the slipway of Anderson, Rigden and Perkins shipyard where Alan was an apprentice. She had two planks stove in and Alan acted as 'boy' to George Richards, the shipwright who undertook the repairs.

Alan did not see her again until 1987, now at Faversham; her owner had sailed up the creek and asked him to do some work on her which he did. A major refit was carried out in the mid 1990s, and she was exhibited at the Wooden Boat Show at Greenwich. The owner intimated that he only bought her to prevent her being sold to American owners, presumably to keep her in this country. He subsequently disappeared, coincidentally to America, abandoning Eel in Alan's yard. Attempts were made to contact him without success; she was therefore left to her own devices and by 2008 was in a very sad state indeed.

Alan could not bring himself to break her up, but storage charges were mounting up with little prospect of payment, so the decision was made to sell her for a nominal sum to a new owner who was committed to restoring her. That owner was Trevor

EEL *by George Holmes*
21ft × 7ft

Pallet, who already had a professionally built and partly completed hull, inspired by Albert Strange's *Cherub II*, He decided that 'owning the real thing, rather than a replica' was a far better thing, so the story of her latest restoration begins.

The first problem to be encountered was that a previous owner had replaced the keel bolts with lengths of mild steel studding The original keel bolts were what is known as 'upset head' bolts, which means a tapered head which fitted in a similarly tapered hole in the ballast keel. He had welded the studding to the ballast keel and as keel bolts are not perpendicular but rather dovetailed outboard at the top the studding had to be cut through in between the wood and iron to remove the external ballast keel. Once removed the full extent of the damage to the wood keel became apparent.

The mahogany keel was split from the centreboard slot forward, passing through the forward keel bolt and the centre line bolt through the forward deadwood. A new iroko keel was fashioned and the old one removed, which entailed removing the garboard planks. The new keel was fitted along with a new lower section of sternpost and the garboard planks re-fitted. The majority of the steam-bent timbers were replaced along with about half of the sawn oak frames.

The original centreboard case had been replaced in the past with a lightweight plywood version, more suitable for a dinghy than a hefty little cruiser, secured with flimsy 1in square battens screwed to the keel. Out it had to come and a new Iroko case, made in accordance with the original drawings, was fitted. Fastened to 3in square bed logs, themselves bronze bolted to the new keel, it is much more workmanlike and now fit for purpose. A couple of new deck beams were made, one incorporating the original registration carving as an inlay, a very nice touch by Alan.

The outside of the hull was sanded back to bare wood and the caulking removed, the gaps between the planking being filled with epoxy. The old deck was replaced with a new one of plywood, epoxy sheathed. The hull and inside of the case are also epoxy sheathed with woven glass cloth, as she is to spend some of her time on the fresh waters of the Norfolk Broads. The interior was also stripped to bare wood and given three coats of water based epoxy.

Sheila, designed in 1903, is the oldest surviving Albert Strange yacht, having celebrated her centenary in 2005. She began life cruising extensively on the West Coast of Scotland, unforgiving waters to say the least, and she finally laid to rest the myth

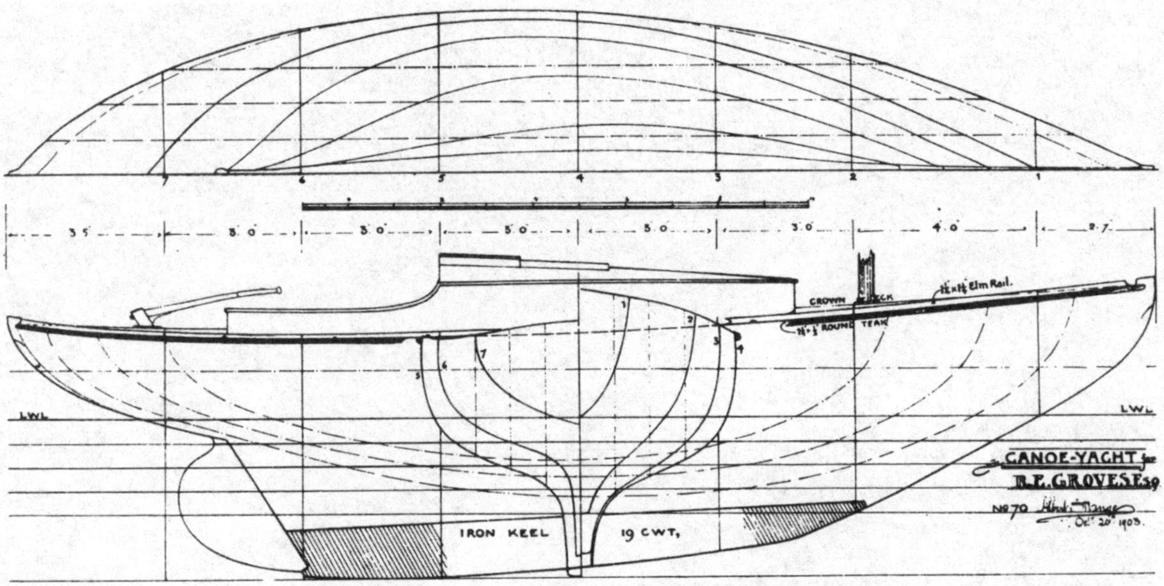

SHEILA
by Albert Strange, lines

of the time that small boats were unsuited to such work. She was named after her owner Robert Groves' first daughter; Groves was an artist and a very colourful character to say the least; he engaged in considerable mischief during his lifetime and was still fathering children aged 72 with a young lady over 50 years his junior. If that is not a good recommendation for ownership of a canoe yawl then I do not know what is.

In the specification published in the 1904 Humber Yawl Club *Yearbook* she was described as follows: 'Although she will not often be sailed single-handed the sails have been kept small enough for easy working by one hand. The deep (too deep!) waters of the lochs and harbours admit any amount of depth of keel, so a centreboard was not made part of the design and the placing of nearly the whole of the ballast outside, at a depth sufficient to give ample stability without seriously effecting the ability of the boat to take the ground, gives excellent floor space and headroom in the cabin.' The specification was for pitch pine planking, ¾in finished, with

SHEILA *by Albert Strange, 25ft × 6ft 9in × 3ft 6in*

1in garboards, elm keel, oak stem, stern post and timbers. These are 2½in × 2½in on the sections shown in the lines, with two steamed elm timbers 1½in × 1in between. The coamings, cabin top and king plank are of teak and the deck of 2½in × ⅞in yellow pine. The cabin plan shows ample locker space and three berths can be arranged (one athwart ship).

One other boat, *Sea Breeze,* was built to the design at that time by the same builder, and possibly another one, this time sloop rigged with 378 sq. ft. of sail for a W. Booth in 1915.

Groves kept *Sheila* for some years, writing extensively on her cruises and, as already shown in Chapter 5, producing delightful illustrations both of her and the Highland scenery he so much enjoyed. Groves was a member of the Humber Yawl Club and when he commissioned Albert Strange to produce a new design, *Sheila II*, *Sheila* passed into the ownership of another HYC Member, Patrick Walsh, an Irishman who rebuilt her in 1914 following her being 'written off' in a storm in Dublin Bay. Coincidentally, Walsh also bought *Sheila II* from Groves when he sold *Sheila* on after the 1914/18 war. *Sheila II* also survives, in New Zealand—sold in 1949 to Adrian Hayter and featured in his classic account of her voyage there, *Sheila in the Wind.*

In the twenties and early thirties *Sheila* led a chequered life, but in 1935 she was bought by James Wilson, a Scot, who owned her until 1978; he sold her and bought her back twice during this time. One of these sales in 1939 resulted in her being hit by a stray bomb whilst in a boatyard in Ayr. Wilson bought her from the insurers for £20, repaired her only to sell her again in 1950, buying her back 5 years later because he did not see her being kept properly. She was bought in 1978 by Mike Burn, who had been badgering Wilson to sell her for 20 years. Mike carried out a couple of restorations over the years and she is now in pristine condition, as befits a lady of her mature years.

She is still sailed without an engine and she handles beautifully with the ease of a sailing dinghy; to watch her dance in and out of moorings under sail, with only the assistance of a pinrail to adjust the helm, is truly a sight to see. Over the years *Sheila* has revealed much about the sailing qualities of the type, one worthy of particular mention is that, despite the comparatively low freeboard, she does not take water into the cockpit even in very turbulent conditions, and following seas are reliably parted by the little canoe counter without driving the bow underwater. She is a well known and a much admired sight in her home at Woodbridge.

Sheila has cruised extensively throughout her long life; she won the Humber Yawl Club premier cruising trophy in 1910 and 1911 for her last two cruises with Groves, and again in 1983, when Mike Burn sailed her from the Deben to the Humber to take part in the HYC Centenary Regatta. Her cruise from the Deben to Douarnenez in 1988 for DZ88, which took 4 days there and 3 days back, won her the cruising trophies of the Old Gaffers Association, The Woodbridge Cruising Club and the Cruising Association.

The only difference in her today compared to when she was launched are the gilding done when Walsh restored her in 1914, including the swept planking on the deck, recreated in 1994 with Alaskan yellow cedar fastened directly to the deck beams, as original practice. She now draws rather more water than the original following the 1914 rebuild for reasons yet to be established for certain, and has an extra stay on the mizzen. Other than that she is as she was, retaining the original deck pump, cabin slide, doors and furniture, and mainsheethorse. The beautiful bronze rudder head bears her name and date, and a plate carries her builder's name and port with the three legs of Man; both elaborate affairs for so small a yacht.

The jib, main and mizzen rigging details are exactly as in 1905. The mizzen boom, like its canoe forbears, is furled with a brail up to the mast so the sail can be 'removed' immediately for stopping. The original reefing jib allows any area to be set and with all the sail control gear, including the throat down haul, being led aft ensures everything, except setting the tack reef hook and hauling the appropriate clew line for a reef, is done from the cockpit, allowing her to continue to tack through tight tidal moorings and sail into marinas with confidence. She was designed to be rowed with sweeps as an alternative means of propulsion and still has the original rowlock bosses on the cockpit coamings. As this book goes to press, *Sheila* has just changed hands, into the care of an experienced sailing instructor based at Morbihan in southern Brittany.

LEONA *by Albert Strange*
24ft × 7ft 5in × 2ft 6in

Leona, built in 1906 by Bundock Bros. of Leigh on Sea, spent the early part of her life on the Thames Estuary. She had five previous owners before she was bought by Jack Wise in 1932, who did away with the original yawl rig and converted her into a sloop. She was sold on in 1936 to Major Penn Curzon of Watermouth Castle in Ilfracombe who carried out further modifications, removing the coal stove, installing a toilet and a two-cylinder Stuart Turner auxiliary petrol engine. After 1946 she disappears from Lloyds lists, reappearing again as *Blue Jay* in 1980.

She was rediscovered by Mike Burn, the owner of *Sheila*, in Topsham, Devon in 1984, and she was subsequently bought by Albert Strange Association member, and boatbuilder, Jamie Clay, who brought her back to Maldon, not very far from where she was originally built and sailed. Fortunately Jack Wise was tracked down and he provided a lines plan and outlined some of her history.

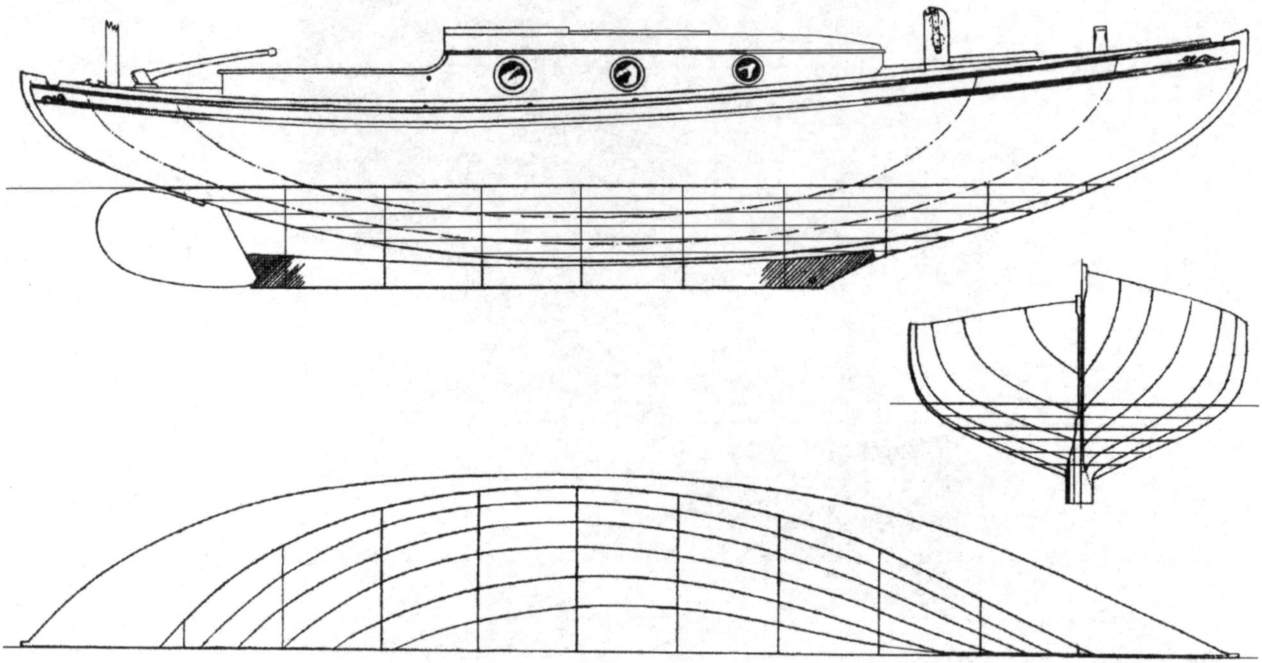

LEONA
after AS #61, lines

There was no clear idea as to the original designer, although successive owners had claimed she was an Albert Strange design. The Bundock Bros. plans made reference to an original design from which she was built, with mention of minor modifications made, such as smaller overhangs at the stem and stern. She is similar to a number of designs by Strange but differed somewhat to all of those known and was previously thought to be a variant of his #40, *Otter*. Whilst researching for this book some years ago, I came across a design by Strange unpublished for more than a century, #63, which is described in detail in Chapter 5.

The centre plate stops below the deck instead of the original lever plate and the cabin has been extended forward, though no mention of these modifications is made on the Bundock plans, otherwise the similarities between the two designs are remarkable. Reproduced on tracing paper the lines plan was overlaid on those of #63, and I can now say with a fair degree of certainty that she was built from this design. Bundock's lines plan was probably copied from those I rediscovered, which were published a few years before in *The Yachtsman*.

Leona was originally built of yellow pine on rock elm. By the 1980s the centreplate had been removed and the slot blocked off, the massive 9in × 3in keelson was rotten, most of her fastenings were gone, including all but one of her keel bolts, and most of the floors and all of the ribs were broken or rotten. There was no coach roof and most of the deck was missing. Moreover two elm bilge pads had caused all the original steamed frames to crack at the intersection along with the remedial doublers and treblers. Not an auspicious start.

The hull was badly distorted so the first job for Jamie was to remove the mid-ship frames and fit a pair of threaded steel tie-rods athwart ships with nuts, washers and wooden bearing blocks, which after some considerable effort with a very large spanner restored the original shape of the increasingly flimsy hull. Six pairs of new frames were then laminated in situ, with the hull suitably braced whilst this was being done. A couple of temporary floors bolted through the now un-blocked centre plate slot completed the job of stabilising the hull.

Due to pressure of work Jamie was forced to part with her, the advertisement in *Classic Boat* magazine being spotted by John May, who purchased her and transported her back to his home near Brough, on the River Humber—the spiritual home of the type. John, a market gardener, put her in a polytunnel to protect her from the inclement Yorkshire weather, and mounted her on a base of railway sleepers. He then embarked on a three-year restoration programme, fitting it between his many other commitments. The first job was to remove the keel: the hull was supported by a mixture of jacks and formers, and when the temporary floors were removed there was only one keel bolt left attached to the hull, so sliding it out proved a much simpler job than anticipated. Alas, the next job was rather more difficult, as the iron keel had to have eleven new holes drilled for bolts, as the original wrought iron ones defied all John's attempts at removal.

A compressor and needle gun was hired and "I gave it a good going over, rust and dust everywhere, me included" as John put it, and he then finished it with epoxy tar.

To remove the wooden keelson the garboards were removed, but the top four planks either side were left in situ to retain the hull shape. The new keelson was formed from a huge 22ft long baulk of 9in × 3in oak cut to shape. A jig was fabricated using a large RSJ as a backbone and the timber steamed for an hour, and then chocked into the jig and left for a week to set. It was then drilled for the new keel bolts, and the centre plate case built and all refixed to the rest of the hull. The ballast keel was now rolled back and bolted to the new keelson with a coat of bituminous mastic to seal the joint.

John then began steaming and replacing the remaining ribs with new ones of 1½in × 1in oak, only one of the originals now remaining. The rebate on the keelson was faired and two new larch garboard planks fitted. Opepe, a dense African hardwood, was used for the new floors fitted between the keel bolts. The cabin was rebuilt as the original drawings indicated, with steamed carlins for the coach roof sides. New deck beams were fitted, and overlaid with 2 layers of ⅜in plywood covered in glass cloth and epoxy to form the new deck.

Laminated coach roof beams were fixed to the curved sides and topped with a laminated plywood roof; the 2 layers of ¼in ply being forced into compound curvature. New spruce masts and spars were built and finished with linseed oil. A new samson post, grab rails, toe rails, rubbing strakes and fore hatch finished the job. In the end John had managed to retain just the stem and stern posts, along with some planking and part of the beam shelf. Complete with a BMW single-cylinder diesel with a side mounting folding prop, *Leona* was finished off in two-tone dark and light blue, which complements her varnished trim very well indeed. Leon has been sailed regularly on the Humber by the Mays until well into their eighties, and in the spring of 2016 she passed into the ownership of Dick Wynne, publisher of this book and current Chairman of the Albert Strange Association, who will keep her on the East Coast.

Mist was built in 1907 and her story is one that often overtakes old boats. A family tragedy left her outside a caring routine, and she sank at her moorings on the Gareloch in Scotland because a neglected swivel had seized and she wound herself under the water. She was lifted in due course, but then lay neglected on the owner's barge. Jim Hill, a local boatbuilder who had originally helped raise her from the loch, managed to persuade her owner not to break her up for scrap, but was then obliged to watch her steady decay over the years, and she was eventually abandoned on a nearby beach. Ever-resourceful, Jim arranged for a local floating crane to lift her and place her inside an abandoned aluminium lifeboat for greater protection from the elements.

At this point a dog-walking local resident spotted *Mist* and put the Albert Strange Association in touch with Jim Hill, and a flurry of activity ensured to save

MIST by Albert Strange, in 2016 and (below) on her recovery in 2006

this historic vessel from destruction. Members of the Association underwrote the costs of getting Mist moved within reach of a road, and Jim built a steel cradle for her eventual recovery. When salvage seemed assured the Secretary arranged for a photo of the derelict, with a write-up, to appear in *Classic Boat* in the hope a new owner would emerge.

Fortune smiled on *Mist* once more and through the involvement of ASA member and Woodbridge resident Mike Burn, Woodbridge boatbuilder John Krejsa saw the picture. Matters of ownership and recovery cost being quickly resolved, *Mist* was transported south in November 2006 to undergo a lengthy and faithful rebuild. John's first appreciation was that *Mist* remained fair; there were no distortions that would need to be pulled back into shape. Her spirit was very much alive, beneath a patina of moss, weed, rot, and ill-advised post-war modification.

John arranged for her to lie in a corner of the yard at Melton, near Woodbridge, Jim's cradle becoming the foundation of a framework to hold her together as work began. Funds were limited but John has always worked to a very tight budget so, where choices are to be made between perfection and a good workmanlike result, the latter would prevail. It was very soon apparent that new frames and a new stem and sternpost were essential so John began the creation of a new set of epoxy-laminated iroko frames built up from 3mm laminations, each frame copied against the original prior to its removal.

Mist was intended for the turbulent waters of the Irish Sea and the Atlantic coast of Ireland but she was rather lightly built, even for the type. Her planking, pitch pine below, mahogany above, was only ⅝in thick and her framing equally light, but now John has beefed up her scantlings a little. It was essential to ensure that her shape was not lost during rebuilding and the steel framework helped here, which John braced with more woodwork.

John drew up a new working drawing from copies of the originals held in the ASA drawing archive. The iron ballast keel is more than worthy of a mention, as it can be seen from the original drawing, and in the flesh, that its sectional shape is faired and splayed downward to continue the hull's wineglass shape, a truly elegant

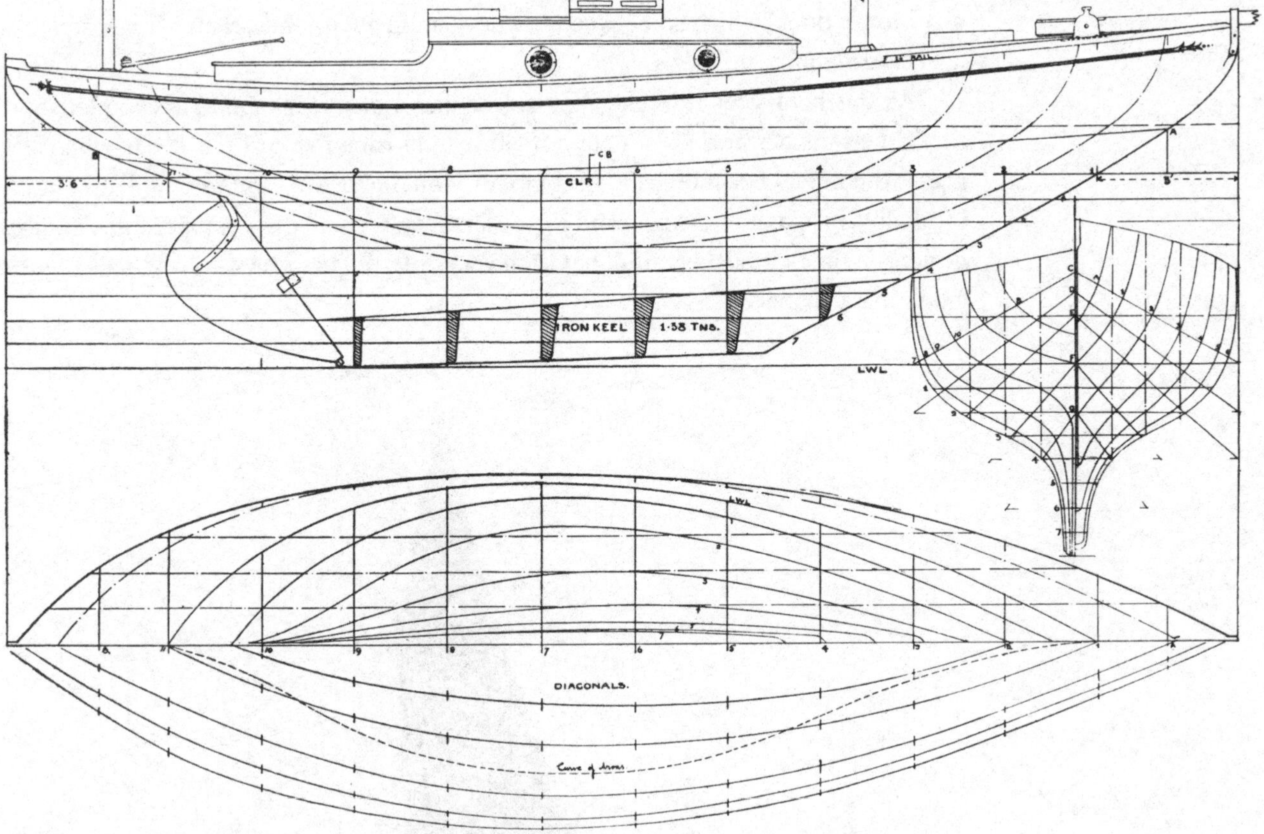

MIST
by Albert Strange, lines

piece of engineering by any standard, and one which distributes its weight to the best advantage.

When the wood keel was inspected it proved to be hard and viable over most of its length, and it was repaired and impregnated with an epoxy made specifically for that purpose. This avoided a very costly replacement, the process of which may have jeopardised *Mist*'s shape. Several keel bolts were replaced, and new stem and stern post laminations were made, and thirteen pairs of new laminated frames fixed, along with a new deadwood knee and laminated counter. Patterns were made *in situ* for new cast bronze floors which sit between the new laminated frames, then her larch planking could commence.

As this book goes to press, *Mist*'s nine-and-a-half-year rebuild is complete and she just awaits her new sails. I am not alone in looking forward to the day when she graces the water once more, and in company with *Sheila* and *Constance*, will give us an invaluable insight into the past and a wonderful opportunity to compare three similar designs of the type, all beautiful, but each very different in its own way. What a photograph that will make.

SNIPPET
by George Holmes

Snippet was designed by George Holmes for his own use, as a successor to *Eel*, in 1912. She too was built by Akester at Hornsea, and Holmes kept her until his death in 1940. After that she spent some time on the Solent, the west coast of Scotland and the east coast of England, ending up in a yard in Woodbridge, where she lay for some time. She was bought by her present owner, Paul Spooner, a yacht designer by trade, and he brought her home to the Solent.

It took him about six months to bring her up to scratch, and he now does a little structural work every year to maintain her in good condition and, as he puts it, uses 'a lot of paint and varnish'. Most frames and fastenings have been replaced but the planking, backbone structure, cockpit coamings and coach roof are original. The original deck planking was replaced by plywood overlaid with pine planking. The interior has been replaced mostly by Paul; some bits of the original rig remain including the tabernacle arrangement which was designed by Holmes and described in some detail at the time.

Paul now cruises her on local waters with his young family but he has taken her as far as the West Country, the Channel Islands and the east coast. She is regularly entered in club pursuit races and local OGA events, she has even taken part in a Round the Island (Wight that is) race.

Nirvana was designed by Albert Strange for a Lieut. Neil Constant in 1914, but although he is known to have survived the Great War he never built to the design. The drawings were published in the *Yachting Monthly* in 1918, sent in by Constant, prompted by Strange's death in 1917. Finally built in 1925, *Nirvana* was the 5th boat owned by A.W. Mooney and she replaced his ten-ton ketch. He wanted a true single-hander and yet a good hefty boat with plenty of accommodation, but as the size was limited by his pocket and the weight of the ground tackle he 'cut himself down' to a boat of nine tons TM.

Mooney redesigned the accommodation and sail plan to suit himself. Strange originally designed an orthodox layout with a twelve-foot fo'c'sle with one cot, a saloon with two cots, the motor under the bridge deck, and no sink in the galley.

Mooney had four berths in two cabins and a substantial chain locker was built forward. He observed that she was 'built of the best of everything' which has no doubt contributed to her longevity. A sign of her times was the Ailsa Craig inboard engine with a dynamo and a battery, serving internal, riding and navigation lighting, and a wireless set with a permanent aerial courtesy of the topmast shrouds.

NIRVANA
by Albert Strange

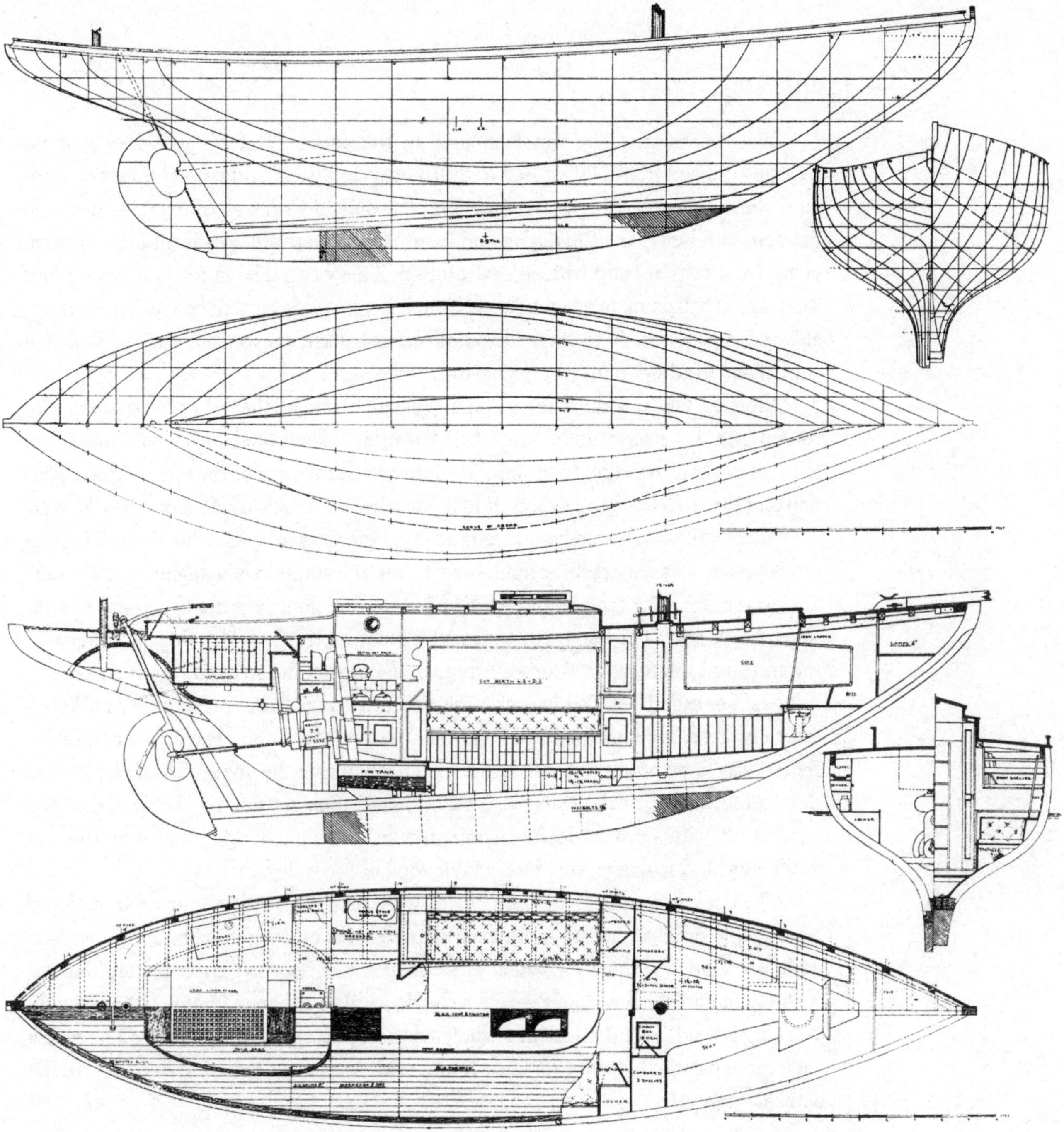

NIRVANA *by Albert Strange, 35ft 6in x 27ft x 8ft 8in x 5ft; sail area 654 sq ft; ballast keel 2.9 tons; TM 8.5 tons.*

Two weeks after she was launched, in the company of his wife and a friend Mooney cruised from Dublin Bay to Stornoway and back, and made cruises of similar distance in succeeding years, including Devon and Cornwall in 1932. He was well pleased with her ease of handling and commented that 'the boat is all I could wish, being fairly fast, dry and with an easy motion. This was not so in the first season, but a change in ballasting made a difference such as one finds hard to believe'. This probably refers to a change to the half-ton of inside ballast, presumably iron pigs, which she carried in addition to the external iron ballast keel.

Mooney had a serious illness in 1933 which forced the sale of *Nirvana*, who passed into the ownership of Mrs Ethel Crimmins; she sailed with a paid hand, but she still cruised the same Irish waters, winning several cups of the Cruising Association and the Irish Cruising Association before the outbreak of the Second World War.

Joe Hamill sold her to her current owner, Pete Clay in 1988, who observed at the time that she was remarkably original apart from the addition of a doghouse and a bermudan mizzen. The table described by Mooney had gone and the heads were amidships, not to port. The epoxy covering had lifted from the deck planking but otherwise she appeared sound, apart from soft spots in the tops of the stem and stern posts.

She was sailed from Whiterock on Strangford Lough to her present base in Woodbridge by Pete, accompanied by his brother, boatbuilder Jamie. Having a boatbuilder aboard was to be propitious, as she sprang a leak during the voyage which Jamie was able to repair. She made a stop at Gareloch, and then set out via the Irish Sea and Lands End, with stops at Howth, Lymington and a couple of other places on the way to Woodbridge, logging a very respectable total of 810 miles.

The deck and most of the deck beams were then replaced and the cabin restored close to the original design. 9mm teak planking was glued to a new 12mm plywood deck, itself glued to the deck beams, all with epoxy. Further extensive restoration was carried out and she now looks very nearly identical to the 1925 photos of her launch. Working abroad, Pete then spent a whole winter of his spare time building a new teak and maple panelled interior for the saloon 'with respectful regard to her 1915 design date' as he puts it.

9 The Canoe Yawl Today

The coastal waters and weather encountered by Albert Strange, George Holmes and their contemporaries are the very same that we experience today, and it follows that the canoe yawl is as well-suited to our needs of a vessel's sailing qualities as it was to theirs. A growing number of owners and builders are responding to this realisation by building new to the old designs, or re-interpreting them for a modern marketplace. I hope their example will finally tempt you to throw off the shackles of convention and become the owner of a canoe yawl.

* * *

Following the rediscovery in the 1980s of the Albert Strange design *Wenda* of 1899, by *WoodenBoat* magazine's Mike O'Brien, the late Phil Bolger, an admirer of Strange, produced lines and construction plans. She has stolen the hearts of many and there is no doubting her slim, haunting beauty and the performance it betokens. Several have now been built and the design continues to attract much interest around the world.

Constance is close to the original *Wenda* design, traditionally and beautifully built. The owner was Dick Wynne who had initially planned to build her himself, but now wanted a robust clinker hull professionally built within a fairly tight budget for him to finish off.

His early fantasy of having the time for a self-built wood-epoxy version soon gave way to realism but now he was concerned about the quality of the plank lining. After viewing a boat called *Molly Cobbler*, built by a Rowhedge, Essex craftsman called Fabian Bush, he knew he had found his builder. He gave Fabian a deceptively clear brief, a boat built to the plans drawn up by Phil Bolger, which would be as faithful to the original as he could devise.

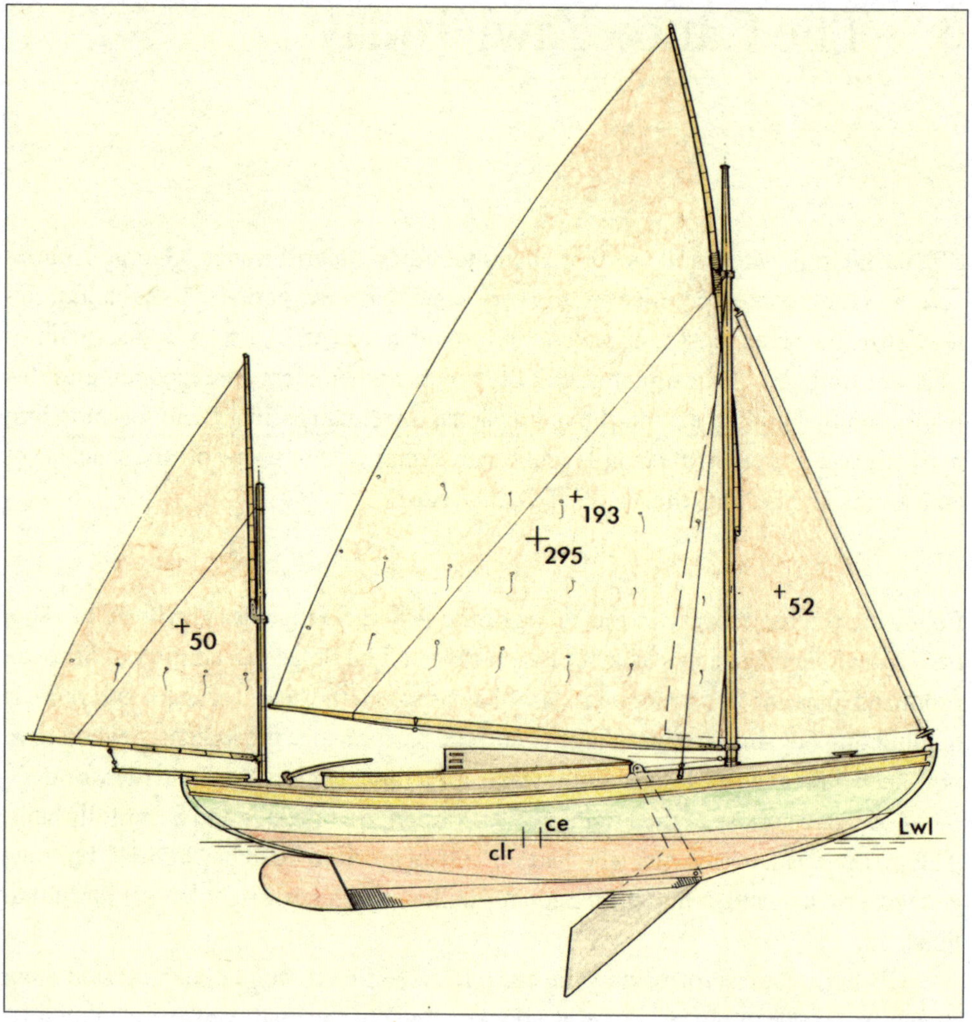

WENDA *by Albert Strange*

The construction agreed upon was relatively thin larch planking on closely spaced oak frames, akin to a beach boat. It soon became clear that, if built to the original lines with scantlings suitable for the intended use—knocking about the shallows

CONSTANCE
to Wenda *by Albert Strange*

of the Thames estuary in the hands of a rookie sailor—the displacement would have to go up. So it was decided to build to the outside of the lines to give the volume to carry the necessary extra weight, and raise her sheer a little to keep her dry. As things turned out she still sat fractionally low in the water for Fabian's liking, but he felt that the changes made had still produced a good boat.

Dick originally wanted an oiled finish to the hull but Fabian argued that it would have some limitations, one in particular was that the planking would need to have more scarf joints to eliminate flaws, knots and waste and keep material costs down. An additional consideration was that a bright finish, once adopted, could not easily be switched to paint; this was because the flush nail-heads of the former could not later be recessed and filled, as would be done when painting. It was finally agreed that paint would look better and offered better protection. Dick feels that there were other details where, but for Fabian's long experience, he might have made the wrong decision.

Fabian is not hidebound by tradition, but Dick wouldn't be persuaded from spruce spars to carbon fibre, feeling that beside departing from tradition, this would alter the boat's motion at sea, and the integrity of the design.

Around this time Phil Bolger called the builder, perhaps *in loco* the designer, urging him to retain the original lines, but Fabian and Dick remained convinced by the rationale they had adopted, and were not the first to have reached the same conclusion.

The sail plan was unchanged from Bolger's drawings, at 275 sq. ft. a little less than the 295 sq. ft. originally drawn by Strange, but boats in the Victorian and Edwardian era were generally somewhat over canvassed by today's standards.

The building started at the end of 2004, and took longer than envisaged. A mutual respect developed and for Dick it was always a pleasure to visit the yard and see creativity and resourcefulness in action; he was as insistent on quality in the details as Fabian was keen to incorporate it, so they were a good match. The partnership was to be tested when Fabian slipped in the yard and broke a leg in three places, putting the project on hold for some time, but throughout this Dick never lost faith.

By now he was busier than ever and came to realise that after all he would be better off if he paid Fabian to finish the boat and get it launched sooner. I had the enormous pleasure of seeing *Constance*, named for Dick's grandmother, launched at the slip across the road from Fabian's yard on a summer's day in 2006, in the company of their respective families and other friends, a smashing day. The following Saturday Fabian and Dick sailed her up and down before the crowd at the annual Rowhedge Regatta, to well-deserved applause.

Her performance, Dick considered, was without doubt 'sparkling' and her slim form proved ideally suited, as the designer intended, to the 'short, steep seas of the Thames Estuary', helping her give larger craft a good run for their money. Her looks drew admiration wherever she went and he never felt the slightest qualm of insecurity

SALLY
derived from Wenda
by Albert Strange

in her, often single-handed in very boisterous conditions, when the 'jib and mizzen' configuration performed exactly as advertised.

Dick's partnership with *Constance* ended when two independent events conspired benignly against them: A friend hoped he would take a half-share, and ultimately full ownership, of his somewhat larger, at 33ft, Albert Strange yawl *Charm.* And a stranger telephoned him to insist on buying *Constance*, whom he had admired for some time, despite being assured by the local yard that the owner would never part with her. The one event facilitated the other, but *Constance* still lives on her old mooring, Dick sees her often, and considers her worth a broken leg of anyone's money.

Sally, like *Constance*, is also based on the *Wenda* design and was built in California towards the end of the 1990s by Jake Roulstone with the help of boat builder Brent Smith. The modifications to the original plans again included building a little larger and deeper so she is of course somewhat heavier as a result, about 4000lbs, which is 600lbs over the original design displacement, not unlike *Constance*. She was also given a different plate arrangement with no lever for the plate inside the boat, so the cabin was extended forward, which is a fairly common modification with that type of centre plate.

She was rigged as a Bermudan yawl instead of the original lug yawl, and the mizzen brought forward to eliminate the bumkin. Clinker planked in ½in glued and clenched plywood on 3½in × 1in sawn frames, she has a plywood deck and moulded plywood for the cabin top. With a couple of watertight bulkheads, oil finish inside and yacht enamel outside, she comes complete with a handsome set of custom made bronze deck hardware. She is an exceptionally pretty boat; the planking looks sweet and is well lined off, a joy to behold.

Eun Na Mara designed by Iain Oughtred illustrates the understandable modern trend towards large volume in a given length, with comcomitant beam and freeboard; with occasional exceptions, design mirrors the market and current fashion. The result may be less seaworthy than more faithful examples of the type, but few modern sailors venture far enough out to sea, or stay there long enough, for this to be a serious concern.

Following is an edited version of Iain's thoughts on her, which I think sum up very well the dilemma facing designers these days.

> “The canoe yawl type was decided upon from the beginning; it makes a particularly pleasant cruising boat, buoyant, sea kindly, shallow in draught with adequate accommodation, and a versatile, seamanlike rig. Always keeping in mind the fundamental requirement for a graceful and well proportioned design, the main problem was to fit in a comfortable cabin and useful cockpit. There followed an exchange of views, the owner demanding more headroom and the designer steadfastly refusing to compromise the appearance of the boat. The final headroom is minimal, but enough.

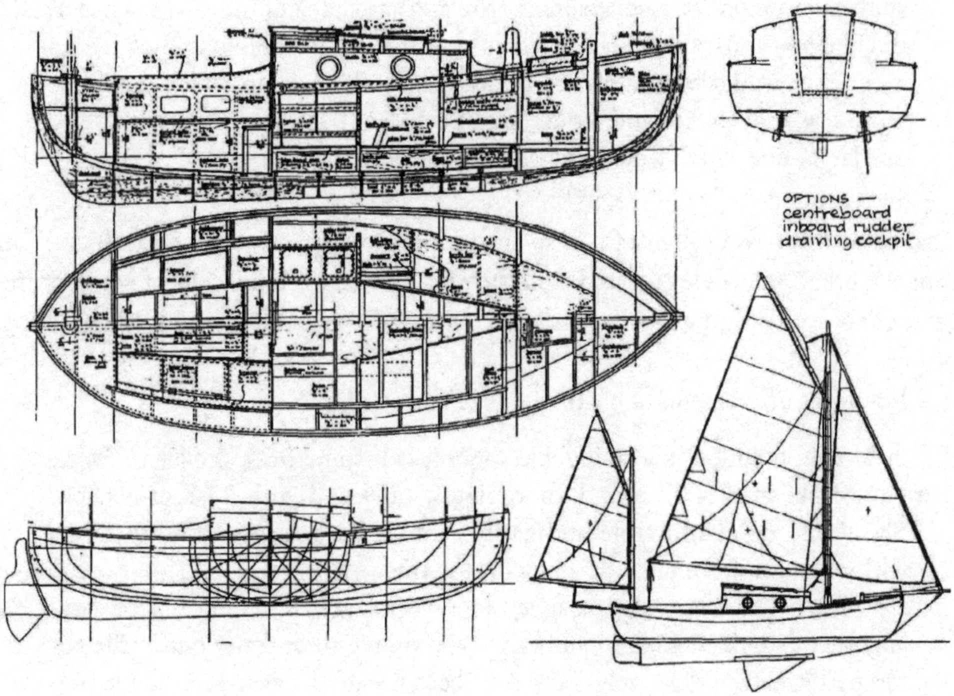

EUN NA MARA
by Iain Oughtred

The disadvantage of shallow draught is the need for a centreboard, and in a boat of this size a case in the middle of a small cabin can be an encumbrance. One solution is the use of twin bilge boards. I felt doubtful about the cost and complication of two cases, plates and lifting gear. The owner was willing to accept these considerations and in a weak moment the builder agreed to put it all together, and I was now free to plan the interior.

To support the weight of the crew and gear it is a full-ended hull, buoyant in the ends with a firm bilge and 500lbs of ballast in the lead keel and the steel bilge boards. The beam is carried well into the ends, and the after body is quite full to provide sufficient buoyancy to support the weight of too many people in the cockpit. Canoe sterns have a way of leaving a clean wake in spite of variations of displacement, trim and sea state. This in a sense makes the hull more adaptable than a transom stern boat; in a hull of limited length a designer would have a choice between a small transom which would be more sea kindly but would reduce the effective WL length and buoyancy aft, or a larger one which would drag when heavily laden.

Teal, also from Iain Oughtred, is a new design freed from the constraints of an owner's brief. She is elegant and well thought out, and reminiscent of some of the early canoe yawls, in particular George Holmes' *Daisy* of 1889 and his later *Ripple* of 1937.

Following are some of Iain's thoughts on her:

"The intention is a trailerable canoe yawl, something similar to *Ripple* but a little smaller all round, more lightly built and with a larger cockpit. She would be comfortable and easily-handled by a crew of one to three, with room for more to come along for the ride.

The sailing rig is the balanced lug and mizzen. This lug is a remarkably seaworthy and user-friendly rig, very simple to operate, quite efficient for performance, relatively very safe because of the way the boom prevents the sail twisting excessively downwind, without the need for a kicking strap. And it can be lowered away quickly. The full-length battens help to keep it quiet when the sheet is eased off, and improve the shape when the wind is on the 'wrong' side. The mizzen is very handy for heaving to, holding the boat head-to wind while hoisting the foresail and balancing the boat under sail.

This same rig was very popular in the canoe yawls and in the smaller light sailing canoes—for all these reasons. There will also be an optional 3-sail rig, with jib, main and mizzen, as *Ripple* has. This is a little more work to set up, with the shrouds and forestay, jib sheets etc. But again it is a seamanlike and versatile rig, as the boat can keep sailing while a reef is tucked into the mainsail in a freshening breeze. In a sudden hard squall the main can be dropped altogether, and she will still be well-balanced, comfortable

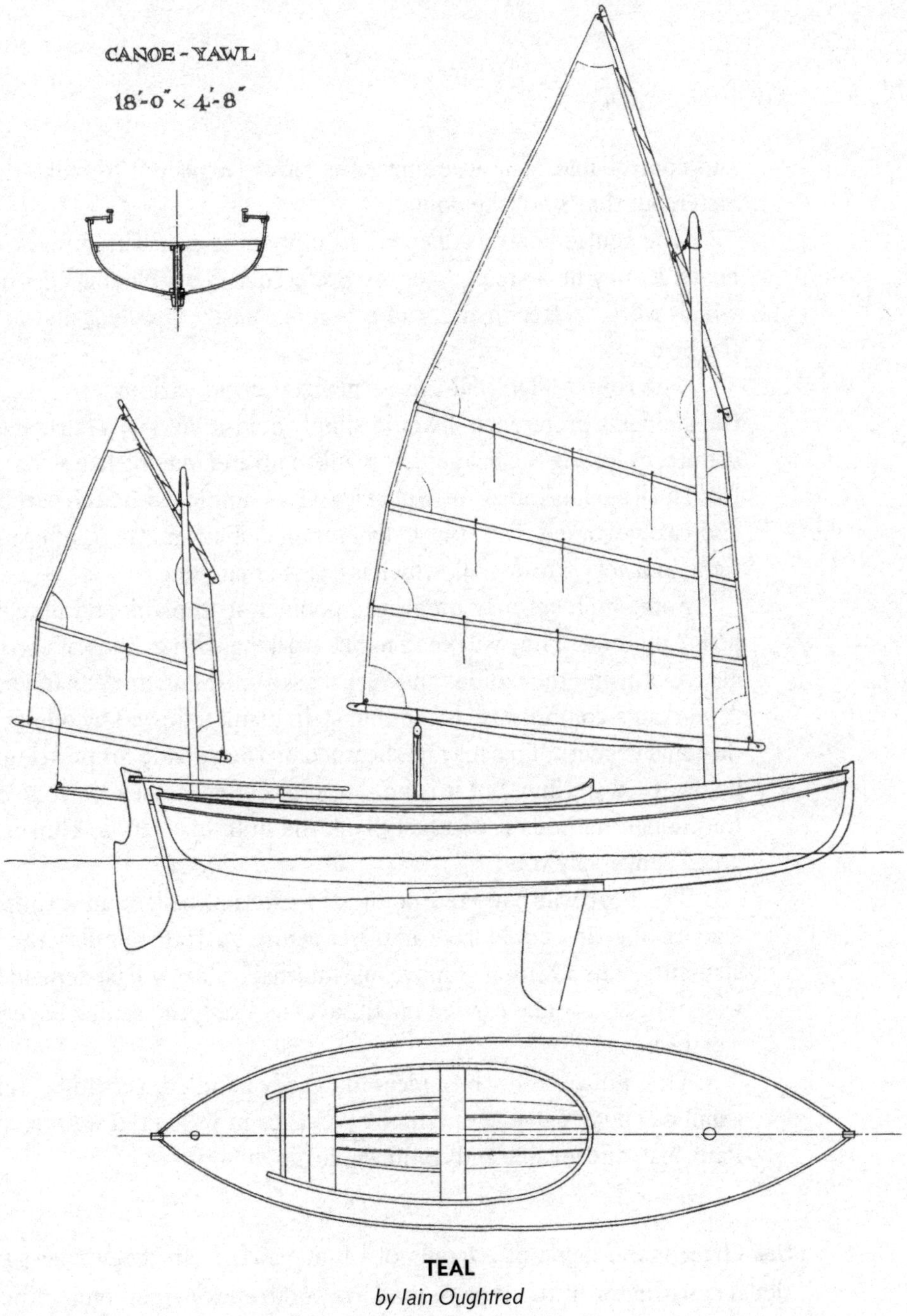

TEAL
by Iain Oughtred

and controllable. The wee mizzen is hardly expected to make the boat go faster, but that's not the point.

The centre board is deeper and more efficient than in many of the old boats. It may be a steel plate; my preference is a well-shaped wood board, which works better in the water, is more easily handled, and is kinder to the boat.

The round-bilge hull can be planked up in various ways, according to the builder's preference. I would simply cold-mould it; a fairly tedious procedure, as having the boat nicely planked up and looking like a boat, you have to do it all again. And again. But at least it is simple, with each part being light and easily-worked. But it is a structurally superb method, offering a clean, tight, and very strong hull, which is easy to maintain.

Some builders may prefer the popular strip-plank-and fibreglass composite method. They will need to like working with gallons of epoxy and the glass cloth, and the tedious and very messy finishing, more than I ever could. A workable compromise is the thin strip plank followed by one or two light diagonal veneers. This may be sheathed on the outside for protection, or just below the waterline, but it is not structurally necessary. Anyone preferring traditional methods can carvel-plank the hull, or even do clinker. Or even glued clinker-plywood.

The boat will have 150 pounds of external ballast, in a simple square lead casting, and could have an offset centre board to simplify the backbone structure. The addition of moveable internal ballast will be dependent on the weight of crew to be carried on an 'average' sail, the sailing waters and the weather.

This will certainly be a pleasant, easily handled, versatile, and efficient small day boat, capable of lengthy passages in protected waters, a practical Raid boat, and an able and comfortable dinghy-cruiser.

Sea Otter is the name of a family of canoe yawls from today's best-known professional constructor of the type in modern wood/epoxy—combining the strength and

SEA OTTER
A 13-foot example by David Moss

beauty of wood with low maintenance. He is David Moss, based at Skippool Creek on the River Wyre in Lancashire. He had always admired the seaworthy shape of the double ender, was delighted by a request to build his first canoe yawl in 1986, and has built a number of them since, ranging in size from 13ft to 25ft. All are built to an exceptionally high standard. Also traditionally, he makes a half model of the boat which alas none of the eventual owners will get to have on their wall at home—because David saws crosswise through the model to obtain the true shape of each section from which to build. As a result, there are no Sea Otter plans.

The largest example is a true canoe yacht: *Puffin*, 25ft, was built in 2002 and based on the Clyde CC One Design described earlier, but with a little extra freeboard plus an inboard engine with hydraulic drive. David also modified the centre plate arrangement, still using a lever but with the extension aft under the bridge deck rather than forward, so that the rest of the plate is below the cabin sole, increasing the accommodation space considerably. He also moved the mast further back and adopted a high peaked gaff sail plan of reduced area, and all the ballast is now outside on the keel rather than a mix of inside and outside as originally designed. She was built of Douglas fir strip planking with a ⅛in mahogany cold moulded skin. Most of her component parts were made in-house by David's team including metal fittings, blocks and rigging.

The rest of his canoe yawls are true to the historic type, being well proportioned with a moderate beam. The largest is the 21ft Sea Otter, whose owner had sailed one of David's 13-footers for some time before ordering a larger boat. She has a 6ft 9½in beam and displaces a little under 4000lbs. She draws 2ft 4½in and has a working sail area of 254 sq. ft. A little smaller is the 18ft Sea Otter, with a beam of 6ft 1in. With the plate up she only draws 1ft 6in and displaces a little under 3000 lbs. She has a working sail area of 210 sq. ft. and is also available as a raised deck version to give increased accommodation space below; alternatively she can be supplied as a ¾-decked day boat. As an open boat the 18ft Sea Otter compares well with Iain Oughtred's new *Teal* design described above.

The 15ft 6in Sea Otter is a day boat available with either lug or gunter rig, the latter with a jib set on a bowsprit. She has a beam of 5ft 6in, draws 10in and has a sail area of 147 sq. ft. It was on this boat that David Moss started to develop his own idea of a canoe stern which is very buoyant in the quarters but hollow on the waterline for a clean exit. Although difficult to build, even with strip planks, it makes for a very fast and able boat, even in a choppy sea. The 13ft baby of the Sea Otter family was David's first canoe yawl build, and one of many modern designs derived from George Holmes' *Ethel* of 1889.

Casco Bay from Paul Fisher is a design worthy of mention in some detail; with a true canoe counter she was designed for a client who wanted a fast, easily handled canoe yawl for use on the Swiss lakes. At 16ft 1in LOA with a 4ft 8in beam and short overhangs she has a stable hull form with an attractive sheer line and well cambered decks. The inboard rudder, mounted in a box, avoids the tiller complications caused by outboard rudders, the very problem which prompted Albert Strange to design his first canoe counter more than a century earlier.

CASCO BAY
by Paul Fisher

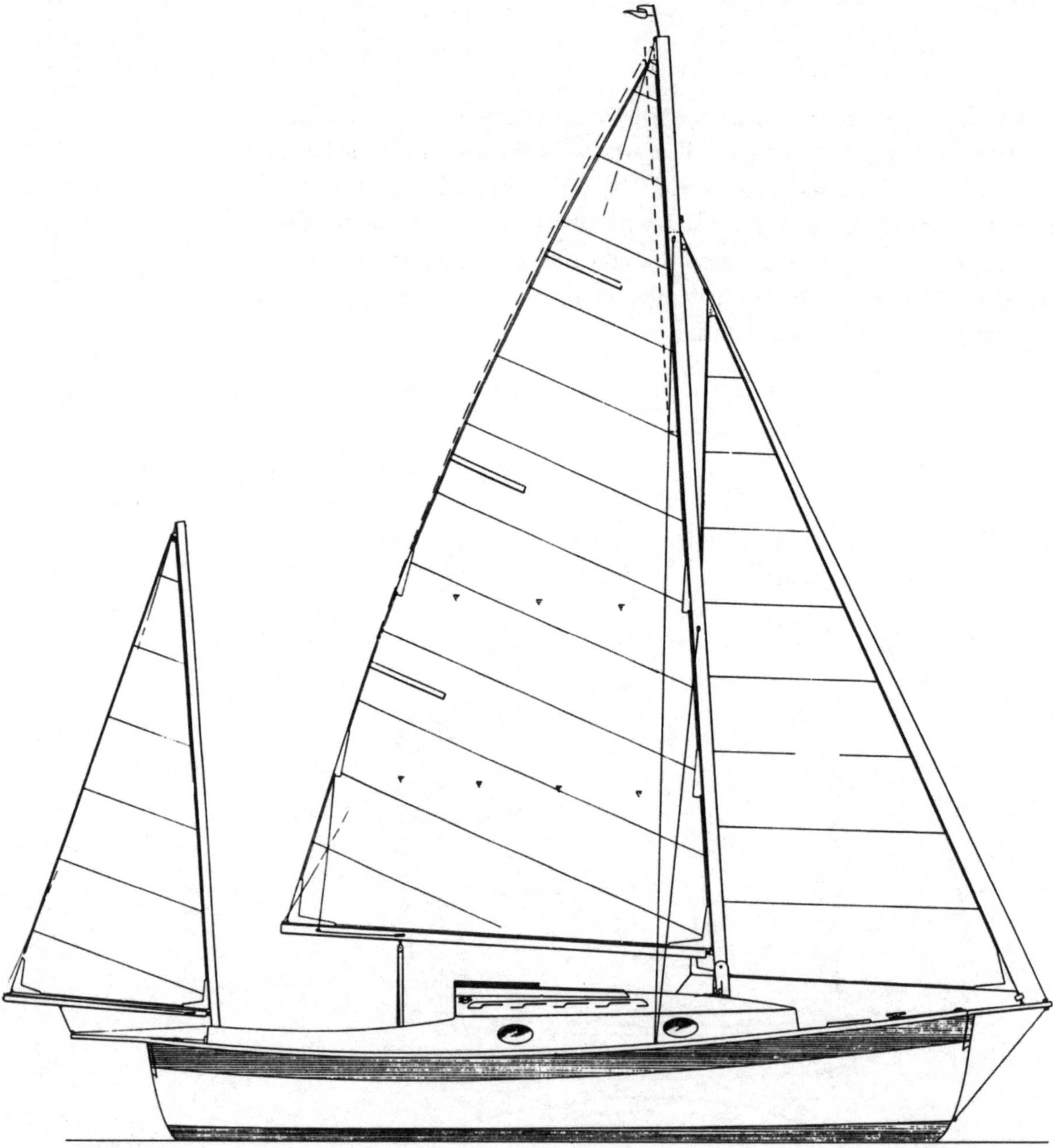

ROB ROY 23, a US-built GRP production canoe yawl designed by Ted Brewer in the 1980s, 23ft x 6ft 9in x 1ft 6in/4ft

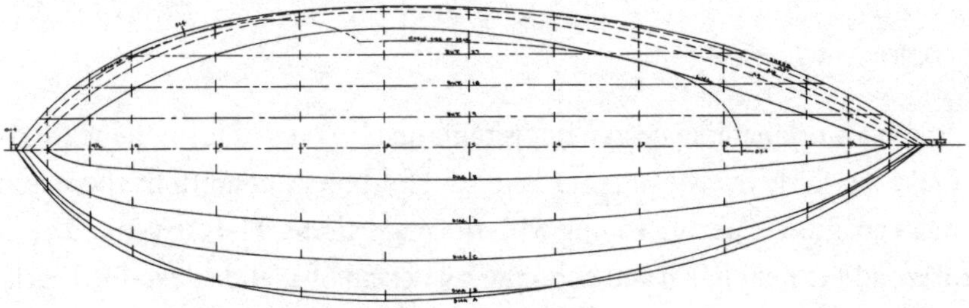

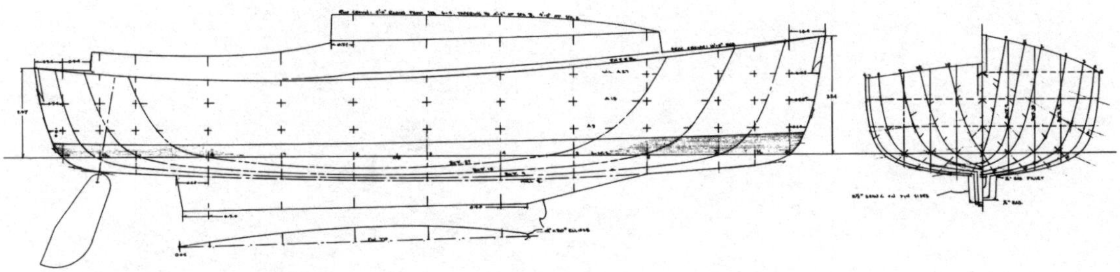

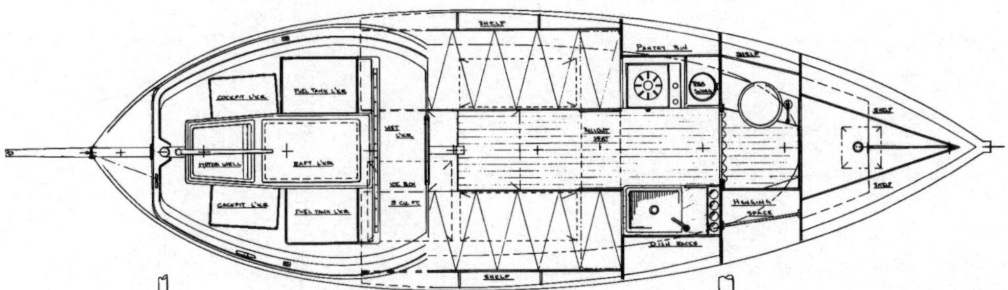
SHELF
PANTRY BIN
SHELF
COCKPIT L'KR
FUEL TANK L'KR
WET L'KR
PULLOUT SEAT
SHELF
MOTOR WELL
RAFT L'KR
ICE BOX
8 CU. FT.
COCKPIT L'KR
FUEL TANK L'KR
HANGING SPACE
SHELF
DISH RACKS
SHELF

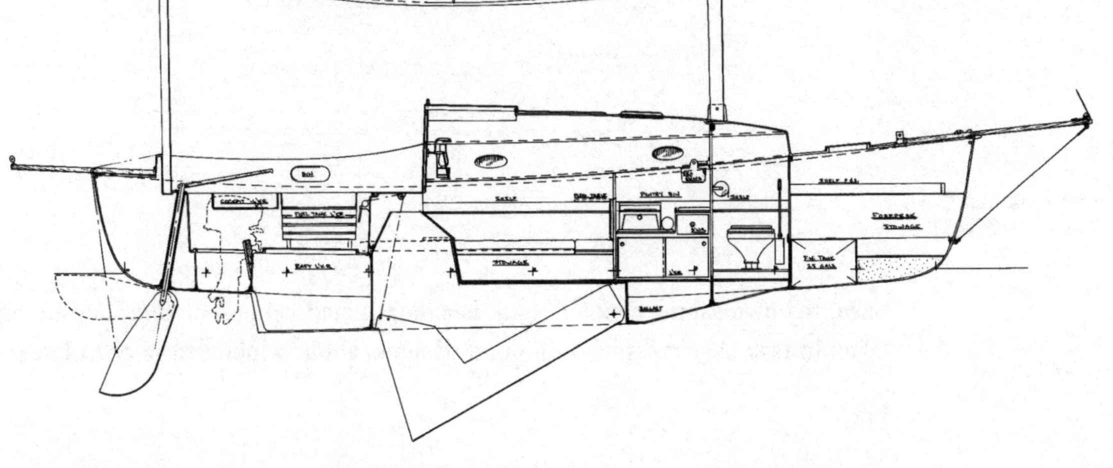
COCKPIT L'KR
FUEL TANK L'KR
RAFT L'KR
SHELF
PANTRY BIN
SHELF
SHELF P&S
FOREPEAK STOWAGE
STOWAGE
BALLAST

She is a workmanlike design but retains an elegance of form, her 140 sq. ft. of sail will make her fairly lively even on a lake, and for breezy conditions there is an alternative mast position to permit sailing with the main alone. The curved spars, though not essential, add to her charm and echo the rig design of Wenda described earlier.

SARA, *sloop version, by Richard Powell*

Sara, my own sailing canoe design, is a lengthened version of *Ethel* and before I am taken to task over messing with good designs, about which I have already expressed my disapproval, may I offer a word in my defence? Small variations on a theme are very much in order and are little different to the natural evolution of the type over a century ago. Another couple of feet would permit more stowage and increase the inbuilt buoyancy as well as reducing the degree of twist at the plank ends making her easier to build.

What I had in mind was something fairly easy to build but still looking pretty without costing a fortune or taking forever to complete. The combination of plywood and strip planking already described achieved this aim beyond even my own expectations. The Bermudan rig had hollow oval strip laminate spars, the mast with mainsail luff rope guide and carbon fibre reinforcement—an indulgence, but just me playing with something I love.

The suggested yawl rig is much simpler than my own sloop rig, and in hindsight a better option. The sails are cut fairly full, the main with a full roach carried high with four battens, the two uppers of which are tapered sailboard battens. My boat proved to be fast and lively without being tender and she moves easily with a whiff of breeze. As I said before, hull design is all and *Ethel*, and this one, are good hulls.

10 A Twenty-first Century Canoe Yawl

A SIGNIFICANT DEVELOPMENT which has boosted the availability of affordable boats in wood is the advent of CNC (computer numerical control) cutting machinery, which has led to a resurgence of interest in kit-built plywood boats. This system also has an application for canoe hulls with a round bilge when combined with strip planking, which I used on my small sailing canoe *Sara*. In my opinion this combination of techniques is worthy of further development; when used with pre-machined timber strips it offers the potential for previously unachievable hull forms in easily-built kits.

Wood composite construction opens up opportunity, but when applied to a traditional design it will result in weight savings of some 30% or more. Therefore the vessel will float several inches too high and require additional ballast. Some of this weight saving will be countered by the provision of 'modern facilities', as the original craft were Spartan by today's standards. Strange at least would have made full use of advances in materials engineering; the need for quality materials a recurrent theme in all his writings.

> “ ...needlessly heavy scantlings... ideas of solidity being carried out, regardless of the fact that every pound of unnecessary wood means one pound less of the necessary lead or iron ballast — *Albert Strange*

Compared with a traditional build, wood composite construction offers enormous scope to incorporate desirable features at reasonable cost, for example: a full curve at the garboards for hydrodynamic efficiency; hull skin thickness varied to take account of the differing loads; high strength-to-weight ratio 'egg crate' ply keel sections and intermediate frames, to reduce deformation on the wind from slamming loads, and

'CY21' *Sail Plan*

minimise bottom failure. The hull and deck can be sheathed with glass for increased resistance to impact and abrasion.

Reinforcement for localised strength is easily and cheaply provided by ply pads at mast steps, shroud attachments, and so on, and by epoxy fillets at structural junctions wherever loads are high. Extra strength is incorporated only where necessary and sufficient for the primary dead, imposed and wind loads, with adequate safety factors. Structural failures are not caused by science, but by bad design, shoddy construction, poor seamanship, or usually a mix of all three, and are not a function of modern construction *per se*.

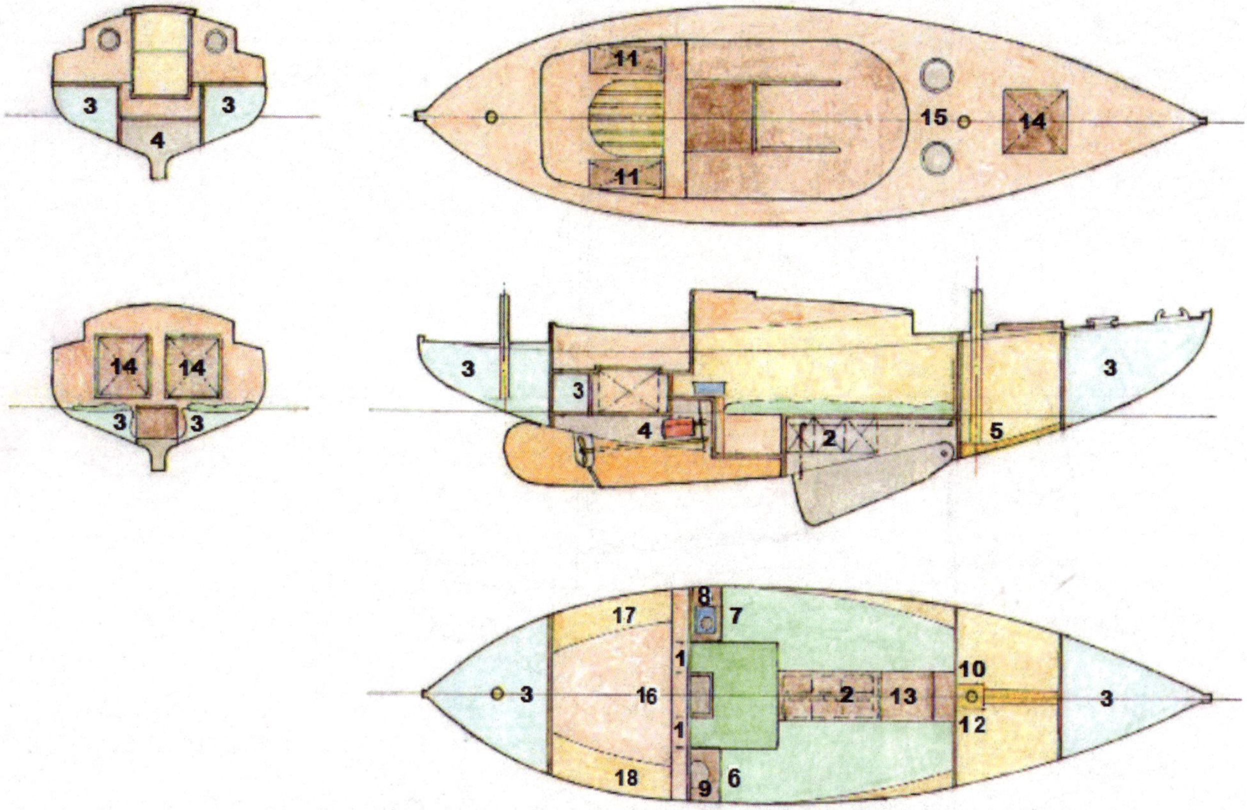

'CY21' *Accommodation*

1 Water containers
2 6 x 6v cells
3 Buoyancy
4 36v electric motor
5 Main anchor
6 Food storage/cool box under sink
7 Utensil storage under cooker
8 Gas cooker
9 Sink
10 Spares
11 Stowage bins under seats
12 Toolbox
13 Chart table, stowage under
14 Hatch
15 Decklights
16 Kedge under deck
17 Lifejackets, oilskins
18 Fenders, mooring warps

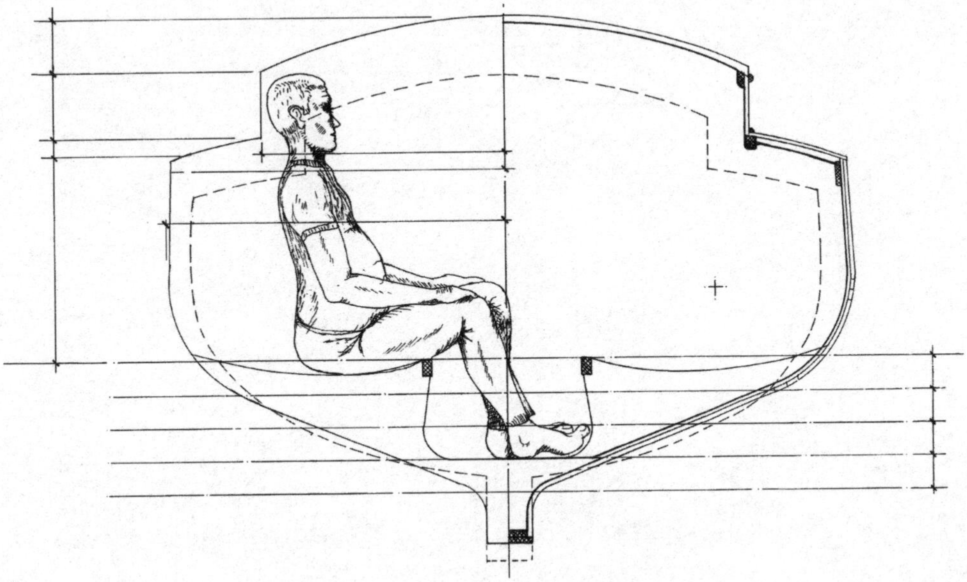

'CY21' *Seating*
Dotted line shows mid-section of Wenda

I have produced a design for a modern wood composite canoe yawl inspired by Albert Strange's enigmatic design number 45, *Wenda*. Employing solid timber, plywood, and modern adhesives and coatings she would be cheaper to build and and easier to maintain than GRP, and a lot more easily and cheaply repaired. Plywood forms her bottom and topsides, with strip-planking of the more curved turn of the bilge.

The good dimensional stability, cross-grain strength and minimal finishing requirement of plywood combine with the strip-planked bilge to offer the best of all worlds in respect of looks, cost and ease of construction. I was pleased to notice that recently a US designer had adopted the idea for one of his boats. Glued clinker plywood would also be nice, but it would require rather more skill.

Working from the inside outwards, the backbone of the boat provides the basis of a building jig, the centreboard case and other fore-and-aft members stiffen it up, forming an armature to which all the other parts are attached. Most plywood sheets are marked out singly and cut double to form port and starboard planks. Some bulkheads

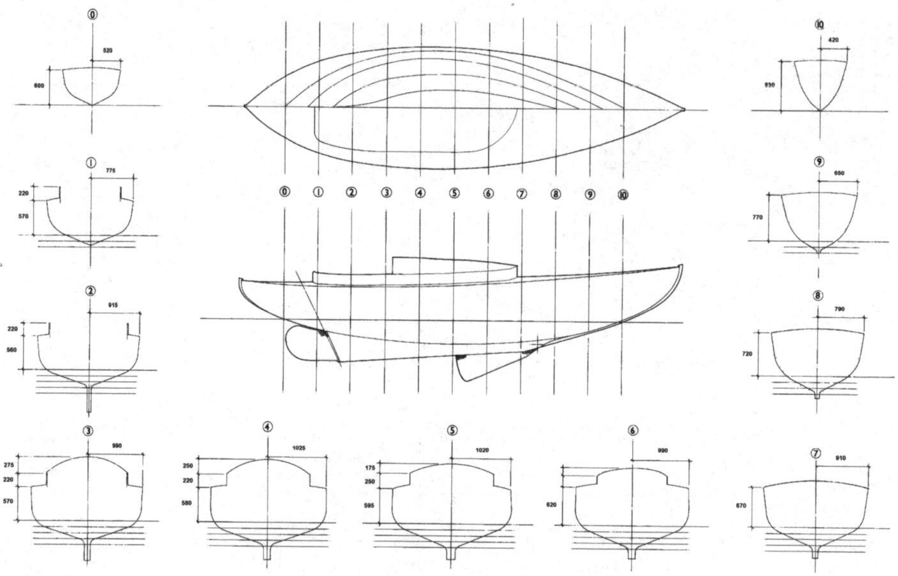

'CY21' *Lines & body plan*

and frames are identical, or nearly so, to reduce the number of patterns required. If the marking out of the hog is correct, and the rake of the keel, then the hull will be true.

I have not changed the basic hull proportions significantly from her antecedents; a seaworthy design is the same now, as then. The first consideration in my fitness-for-purpose evaluation was size. I had intended to build her for my wife and I to sail together and she was to be kept in a marina berth for day and weekend sailing in summer, with winter storage ashore. Berthing rates seem to jump at around eight metres or so, or twenty-six feet. I developed a midship section to provide sitting head-room for two people of modest proportions such as we. An assessment of volume for two snug berths, along with space for simple cooking and washing facilities, in a canoe hull gave me a length of around twenty-five feet overall.

For a given amount of accommodation the canoe hull form will be longer and slimmer than others, leading to higher berthing costs when these are generally based on length. But this is a price worth paying for performance and beauty.

The next consideration was draught and keel type; at the time we lived by the River Crouch on the English East Coast, so shallow draft with a centre board made sense. I have to say, even though we now live in Devon with access to deep water, I would still make the same choice for the sheer flexibility it offers. In addition to the deep waters here there are many picturesque bays, estuaries and rivers to explore which would otherwise be denied to a craft of this size.

I chose lead shot internal ballast, in bags which could be removed to make launching and recovery easier. This worked well on my old gaff yawl and has the advantage of being adjustable to balance the fore and aft trim if required.

Lightweight equipment and ease of handling is paramount. A small hatch forward of the mast would obviate the need to go on deck when anchoring, and a composite centre board would be much cheaper and easier to operate than a steel lever plate. The removal of the lever also enables an increase in cabin space and a slightly larger cockpit.

Auxiliary propulsion by way of sweeps, or indeed a quarter-mounted outboard engine, are possible, though not for me, as nothing does for me quicker than rowing or pulling on a starter cord; also the stowage of sweeps or an outboard can be a problem. The answer for me is an electric inboard engine; this is a more expensive option, but having kept everything else to bare essentials a little indulgence seems merited. The motor is well inboard and the batteries, centrally positioned well down, will act as ballast, reducing the quantity of lead shot.

With a fine run of hull at the ends it is particularly important to keep weight out of them, to ensure that she does not bury herself in waves in heavy weather. The stowage and equipment layouts have been designed with this in mind—weight distribution is an important consideration in canoe yawl sailing. Keep only the bare essentials on board, the other clutter can be left in the garage or better still sent to a boat jumble.

The hull form arrived at by the Victorians is scarcely open to improvement, but this is not the case with the rig, thanks to modern lightweight materials and our greater understanding of aerodynamic efficiency.

The masts and spars are hollow timber, in keeping with the light but strong hull construction, and could be built using a profiled timber strip system of my own devising which has been proven in a number of boats. I have also been developing an affordable carbon fibre / timber composite system using 1.5 mm carbon tube and 1.5 mm Douglas fir veneers; the weight savings are considerable, some sample sections have glued up well, and the cost is reasonable.

The choice between gaff, lug and Bermudan rig will have no definitive outcome as long as there is beer to be drunk; each has its stronger and weaker points, and aesthetics plays a significant part in the decision. As with many artefacts, we are most likely to succeed with that which we find the most appealing; there is no definitive best rig type. Were I younger and fitter my choice would be gaff or lug for the main, but today it would be Bermudan. Whatever the choice, a high-aspect or high-peaked main would be appropriate, to maximise upwind efficiency and minimise boom length. The boat's overall length is sufficient not to need the complication or expense of a bowsprit.

Compared to *Wenda* my concept boat has a little extra draught to compensate for internal, rather than external ballast; the full sitting headroom impacts on the 'trademark' sheer line and is difficult to incorporate, but longer overhangs mitigate this effect. The cockpit, free from the hazard of an overlong boom, is uncluttered; the integral seating provides additional buoyancy and incorporates stowage lockers. Sail and centreboard handling lines are all led back to the cockpit, reducing the need to go on deck.

I have made maximum use of modern materials in this exercise and, with three boats under my belt, two of which were subject to a low level of care for various reasons, I have been able to use my experience to improve my boatbuilding methods and learn from several mistakes, and my materials and finishes reflect this learning curve. The scantlings for canoe yawls have historically been rather light, certainly considerably less than Lloyds, reflecting their relatively modest rig and lower stress overall than the conventional sloop or cutter. The planking on Albert Strange's *Mist* was only ⅝in thick, perhaps slightly less. My design is no exception to this rule.

Wenda, and Albert's design #63 which is quite similar, had displacements in the region of 1.5 tons, so my modern lighter-weight version should be in the region of 1.3 tons; she is of similar dimensions but with a little larger volume. The lower weight will reduce the wetted surface area and should make her potentially a little faster than her predecessors. I have tried to improve her sea-keeping qualities by tailoring her hull with close attention to stability curves, and incorporating as many desirable design elements as possible.

I looked at the question of stowage as an integral part of the design, as was often the practice historically. A little thought at this stage will help to keep the weight out of the ends and as low as possible, both of which will help you to obtain the maximum benefit from the sea-keeping qualities and the internal accommodation of whatever boat you sail.

Index